JOE
LOUIS

JOE LOUIS

Robert Jakoubek

Senior Consulting Editor
Nathan Irvin Huggins
Director
W.E.B. Du Bois Institute for Afro-American Research
Harvard University

CHELSEA HOUSE PUBLISHERS
New York   Philadelphia

Chelsea House Publishers
Editor-in-Chief   Nancy Toff
Executive Editor   Remmel T. Nunn
Managing Editor   Karyn Gullen Browne
Copy Chief   Juliann Barbato
Picture Editor   Adrian G. Allen
Art Director   Maria Epes
Manufacturing Manager   Gerald Levine

Black Americans of Achievement
Senior Editor   Richard Rennert

Staff for JOE LOUIS
Deputy Copy Chief   Mark Rifkin
Editorial Assistant   Leigh Hope Wood
Picture Researcher   Alan Gottlieb
Assistant Art Director   Loraine Machlin
Designer   Ghila Krajzman
Production Manager   Joseph Romano
Production Coordinator   Marie Claire Cebrián
Cover Illustration   Bruce Weinstock

7   9   8   6

Library of Congress Cataloging-in-Publication Data

Jakoubek, Robert E.
    Joe Louis : heavyweight champion / Robert E. Jakoubek.
      p.   cm.—(Black Americans of achievement)
    Includes bibliographical references.
    Summary: A biography of Joe Louis describing his youth in a
Detroit ghetto, his rise to heavyweight champion and major sports
hero, and his role in destroying the myth of racial inferiority.
    ISBN 1-55546-599-4
        0-7910-0244-6 (pbk.)
    1. Louis, Joe, 1914–1981—Juvenile literature.   2. Boxers
(Sports)—United States—Biography—Juvenile literature.
[1. Louis, Joe, 1914–1981.   2. Boxers (Sports)   3. Afro-
Americans—Biography.]   I. Title.   II. Series.
GV1132.L6J35 1990   89-48677
796.8'3'092—dc20   CIP
[B]   AC

*Frontispiece: Joe Louis and his
first wife, Marva, walk along a
New York City street in 1935.*

CONTENTS

On Achievement   7
Coretta Scott King

1
June 22, 1938   11

2
"Man, Throw That Violin Away!"   27

3
"You Gotta Knock 'Em Out"   39

4
The Brown Bomber   51

5
"Chappie, This Is It"   65

6
"The Bum of the Month Club"   79

7
"On God's Side"   93

8
"Save Me, Joe Louis"   105

Appendix: Professional Fight Record   122

Chronology   123

Further Reading   124

Index   125

BLACK AMERICANS OF ACHIEVEMENT

Ralph Abernathy
civil rights leader

Muhammad Ali
heavyweight champion

Richard Allen
religious leader and social activist

Louis Armstrong
musician

Arthur Ashe
tennis great

Josephine Baker
entertainer

James Baldwin
author

Benjamin Banneker
scientist and mathematician

Amiri Baraka
poet and playwright

Count Basie
bandleader and composer

Romare Bearden
artist

James Beckwourth
frontiersman

Mary McLeod Bethune
educator

Blanche Bruce
politician

Ralph Bunche
diplomat

George Washington Carver
botanist

Charles Chesnutt
author

Bill Cosby
entertainer

Paul Cuffe
merchant and abolitionist

Father Divine
religious leader

Frederick Douglass
abolitionist editor

Charles Drew
physician

W.E.B. Du Bois
scholar and activist

Paul Laurence Dunbar
poet

Katherine Dunham
dancer and choreographer

Marian Wright Edelman
civil rights leader and lawyer

Duke Ellington
bandleader and composer

Ralph Ellison
author

Julius Erving
basketball great

James Farmer
civil rights leader

Ella Fitzgerald
singer

Marcus Garvey
black-nationalist leader

Dizzy Gillespie
musician

Prince Hall
social reformer

W. C. Handy
father of the blues

William Hastie
educator and politician

Matthew Henson
explorer

Chester Himes
author

Billie Holiday
singer

John Hope
educator

Lena Horne
entertainer

Langston Hughes
poet

Zora Neale Hurston
author

Jesse Jackson
civil rights leader and politician

Jack Johnson
heavyweight champion

James Weldon Johnson
author

Scott Joplin
composer

Barbara Jordan
politician

Martin Luther King, Jr.
civil rights leader

Alain Locke
scholar and educator

Joe Louis
heavyweight champion

Ronald McNair
astronaut

Malcolm X
militant black leader

Thurgood Marshall
Supreme Court justice

Elijah Muhammad
religious leader

Jesse Owens
champion athlete

Charlie Parker
musician

Gordon Parks
photographer

Sidney Poitier
actor

Adam Clayton Powell, Jr.
political leader

Leontyne Price
opera singer

A. Philip Randolph
labor leader

Paul Robeson
singer and actor

Jackie Robinson
baseball great

Bill Russell
basketball great

John Russwurm
publisher

Sojourner Truth
antislavery activist

Harriet Tubman
antislavery activist

Nat Turner
slave revolt leader

Denmark Vesey
slave revolt leader

Madam C. J. Walker
entrepreneur

Booker T. Washington
educator

Harold Washington
politician

Walter White
civil rights leader and author

Richard Wright
author

ON
ACHIEVEMENT

———⟨∙⟩———

Coretta Scott King

Before you begin this book, I hope you will ask yourself what the word *excellence* means to you. I think that it's a question we should all ask and keep asking as we grow older and change. Because the truest answer to it should never change. When you think of excellence, perhaps you think of success at work; or of becoming wealthy; or meeting the right person, getting married, and having a good family life.

Those important goals are worth striving for, but there is a better way to look at excellence. As Martin Luther King, Jr., said in one of his last sermons, "I want you to be first in love. I want you to be first in moral excellence. I want you to be first in generosity. If you want to be important, wonderful. If you want to be great, wonderful. But recognize that he who is greatest among you shall be your servant."

My husband, Martin Luther King, Jr., knew that the true meaning of achievement is service. When I met him, in 1952, he was already ordained as a Baptist preacher and was working toward a doctoral degree at Boston University. I was studying at the New England Conservatory and dreamed of accomplishments in music. We married a year later, and after I graduated the following year we moved to Montgomery, Alabama. We didn't know it then, but our notions of achievement were about to undergo a dramatic change.

You may have read or heard about what happened next. What began with the boycott of a local bus line grew into a national movement, and by the time he was assassinated in 1968 my husband had fashioned a black movement powerful enough to shatter forever the practice of racial segregation. What you may not have read about is where he got his method for resisting injustice without compromising his religious beliefs.

He adopted the strategy of nonviolence from a man of a different race, who lived in a distant country, and even practiced a different religion. The man was Mahatma Gandhi, the great leader of India, who devoted his life to serving humanity in the spirit of love and nonviolence. It was in these principles that Martin discovered his method for social reform. More than anything else, those two principles were the key to his achievements.

This book is about black Americans who served society through the excellence of their achievements. It forms a part of the rich history of black men and women in America—a history of stunning accomplishments in every field of human endeavor, from literature and art to science, industry, education, diplomacy, athletics, jurisprudence, even polar exploration.

Not all of the people in this history had the same ideals, but I think you will find something that all of them have in common. Like Martin Luther King, Jr., they all decided to become "drum majors" and serve humanity. In that principle—whether it was expressed in books, inventions, or song—they found something outside themselves to use as a goal and a guide. Something that showed them a way to serve others, instead of living only for themselves.

Reading the stories of these courageous men and women not only helps us discover the principles that we will use to guide our own lives but also teaches us about our black heritage and about America itself. It is crucial for us to know the heroes and heroines of our history and to realize that the price we paid in our struggle for equality in America was dear. But we must also understand that we have gotten as far as we have partly because America's democratic system and ideals made it possible.

We are still struggling with racism and prejudice. But the great men and women in this series are a tribute to the spirit of our democratic ideals and the system in which they have flourished. And that makes their stories special and worth knowing. ✤

JOE
LOUIS

1

JUNE 22, 1938

❧

B Y ABOUT NOON, the crowd gathered outside the entrance to Madison Square Garden in New York City was more than the sidewalk could hold. Scores of people spilled into the street and partially blocked traffic.

At around one o'clock, there rolled into view a dark blue Buick escorted by the motorcycles of three state troopers. As this little procession crept along West 49th Street, everyone in the Wednesday afternoon crowd began to stir because they knew that in the limousine's backseat was Joe Louis, the heavyweight champion of the world, and that very night he would be climbing into a boxing ring for the prizefight of his life. Although he was coming to the Garden only for the weigh-in—the fight itself was not scheduled for another 9 hours, at Yankee Stadium, miles away—the throng at 8th Avenue and 49th Street treated the 24-year-old boxer's arrival like the main event. When the long-hooded car finally stopped and one of its rear doors swung open, the cheering could be heard blocks away.

Several men piled out of the car, but no one mistook any of them for the champion. He was a young, light-complected black man, with broad shoulders, a silent, respectful manner, and an easy, loping walk—and, as always, he was handsomely dressed. On this day, he had on a perfectly fitted light gray, windowpane-plaid double-breasted suit and a pale yellow shirt with a soft open collar. A polka-dotted silk scarf was knotted loosely around his neck.

Perhaps the greatest fighter of all time, Louis was the first black American to attain the status of national hero. He secured his place in the limelight in 1937, when he became the youngest heavyweight champion in the history of professional boxing.

11

Louis enters Madison Square Garden in New York City on June 22, 1938, to weigh in for his second fight against Max Schmeling. "Tonight," Louis was quoted as saying in a nationally syndicated article, "I not only fight the battle of my life to revenge the lone blot on my record, but I fight for America against the challenge of a foreign invader, Max Schmeling. This isn't just one man against another or Joe Louis boxing Max Schmeling; it is the good old U.S.A. versus Germany."

On his head, at a slight angle, he wore a white summer straw hat that had a wide black band around the base of its high crown. Clothes were important to the champion. During the next year, he would hang 20 new suits in his closet, purchase 36 shirts and 2 tuxedos, and hire several tailors to craft his personal designs for trousers, lapelless suit coats, and camel hair jackets with leather piping.

Louis was dressed for an outing, but he was all business. He passed through the excited spectators, barely acknowledging their cries of "Good luck, Joe." Inside, he went to a dressing room, where he stripped to his boxing trunks, put back on his pearl gray suede oxfords that went so well with his suit but looked faintly absurd with shorts, and, surrounded by his seconds, headed into the runway that led to the Garden's main floor. There, under a bright, grayish light, nearly 700 reporters—10 times the number that covered presidential press conferences and nearly as many as attended national political conventions—milled about, smoking, speculating, joking, all of them awaiting the casual ritual of 2 fighters, one after the other, weighing themselves on a big Toledo scale.

Also there, and getting impatient because he had been standing around for nearly a half hour, was the challenger, a 32-year-old German with a dark beetle brow and a menacing scowl, the former heavyweight champion of the world, Max Schmeling. Two years earlier, almost to the day, Schmeling had done what every other fighter could only dream about: On June 19, 1936, in the 12th round at Yankee Stadium, he had knocked out Joe Louis.

There was no sense in Schmeling's victory. Louis was eight years younger and the superior fighter. But Schmeling had noticed Louis's bad habit of dropping his left hand too low after throwing a jab, and the German seized this as an invitation for his one overwhelming weapon: a right-handed punch that arrived with the force of a pile driver. Schmeling's right sent Louis to the canvas.

The defeat hardly damaged Louis's career. He learned to train harder and never again underestimate any opponent, and these lessons paid like a bank. In the early summer of 1937 at Comiskey Park in Chicago, he got his shot at the title and made the most of it, demolishing James J. Braddock in eight rounds and becoming, after Jack Johnson, only the second black to hold the heavyweight championship.

But there was the one blot on Louis's record. Champion or not, the loss to Schmeling embarrassed him painfully, and he refused to consider the title altogether his until he avenged it.

In the Garden, as Louis and his entourage neared the scale, the assembled reporters strained to notice the smallest detail, one observing that the champion's beard seemed a little heavier than usual, another detecting a slight swelling under his right eye. For all the hoopla, when the two fighters actually came face to face there was almost nothing to see. Louis kept

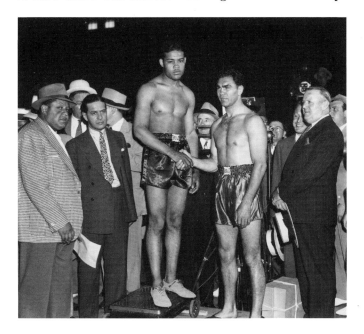

Louis and Max Schmeling shake hands at the weighing-in ceremony before their second fight. "I am a fighter, not a politician," the German boxer maintained during the weeks leading up to the bout. "I am no superman in any way." Despite these denials, the American press depicted Schmeling as a supporter of German chancellor Adolf Hitler's racial supremacy policies.

his head down. Schmeling, in heavily accented English, said, "Hello, Joe," and Louis mumbled a word or two in reply.

Officials of the New York Athletic Commission took their measurements and weights. Both were fine specimens: Louis, 6 feet tall and 198¼ pounds; Schmeling, just as tall and 193 pounds. The weigh-in over, both left, Louis for Harlem, Schmeling for his suite at the Commodore Hotel in midtown Manhattan.

The challenger seemed confident. "Two years ago I knocked him out. Why shouldn't I do it again," he said. Max Baer, another heavyweight, warned that the German "has a great right hand. He is always dangerous. He can murder you." Still, Louis was the clear favorite; the betting odds stood 9–4 in his favor.

Schmeling's underdog status might have made him the crowd favorite because his ring career had the makings of a tremendous popularity. A pleasant, decent man, he had been heavyweight champion from 1930 until 1932, winning as well as losing the title in bouts engulfed by controversy. Afterward, he looked to all the world to be another washed-up fighter.

Somehow, he turned matters around. With his famous right hand pounding away, Schmeling began beating opponents he had once lost to, and with his amazing knockout of Louis he completed what a poll of sportswriters named "the best comeback of 1936." Only one thing marred this appealing saga, and it was the company he kept. Schmeling had become such a favorite of Chancellor Adolf Hitler's that Nazi Germany had promoted the fighter into a symbol of the Third Reich.

At Berchtesgaden, in the German Alps, Hitler planned to stay up into the early morning to listen to the broadcast of Schmeling's fight with Louis. The führer appreciated boxing. "No other sport," he had

Louis's first fight with Max Schmeling: The German boxer raises his arms in triumph as referee Arthur Donovan bends over a stunned Louis and signals the end of the bout. This June 19, 1936, contest marked the first time in Louis's professional career that he had been sent to the canvas.

written years earlier, "is its equal in building up aggressiveness, in demanding lightninglike decision, and in toughening the body in steely agility. Naturally in the eyes of our intellectuals this is regarded as wild. But it is not the duty of a race-Nationalist state to breed colonies of peaceful aesthetes and physical degenerates."

Nor was it the duty of the "race-Nationalist state" to tolerate personal freedom, democracy, representative government, or any person or thing considered "un-German." Beginning in January 1933, when he came to power, Hitler set about building a "new Germany"—a Third Reich that, he prophesied, would last a thousand years. At its foundation was racial hatred, directed most notably against Jews but also aimed at Slavs, Celts, Africans, and the "mongrels" found in the Americas. By 1938, Germany had become a police state, its Jewish residents stripped of their property and legal standing and herded by the thousands into miserable concentration camps.

It soon became apparent that the Nazis wished to rule the rest of Europe and perhaps the whole world. In the spring of 1938, Germany annexed neighboring Austria and immediately began to threaten Czechoslovakia. By September, the continent would be at the edge of war.

Who better to represent the new Germany's athletic valor than the barrel-chested heavyweight with the punishing right, Max Schmeling? During the time he was struggling in the ring, the Nazis had no use for him. But as soon as he defeated Louis in 1936, Hitler could not embrace him fast enough. Right after the fight, the führer cabled Schmeling congratulations for his "splendid victory" and dispatched a giant bouquet of flowers to the boxer's wife, the actress Anny Ondra. A recording of the blow-by-blow account of the fight was played incessantly on German radio, and the state-controlled press traced Schmeling's comeback to the inspiration of a meeting with Hitler: "From that moment on his will to victory was boundless."

When Schmeling returned to Germany in the dirigible *Hindenburg*, the world's largest airship, Hitler had him to lunch. Later, they sat together and watched the film of the fight, the führer slapping his thigh with pleasure every time Schmeling landed a punch.

Poor Schmeling. He was no Nazi. He had little interest in politics and possessed none of Hitler's violent hatreds. But like most ordinary, patriotic Germans, he obediently deferred to the führer. If the Nazis required a symbol, Schmeling would oblige.

For militant, frenzied Germany, then, the prizefight on June 22, 1938, was Max Schmeling, Aryan superman, against Joe Louis, American Negro, a savage representative of what the Nazis considered an inferior race. Before the fight, Schmeling received a cable: TO THE COMING CHAMPION OF THE WORLD, WISHING YOU EVERY SUCCESS. —ADOLF HITLER.

The mere thought of Nazi Germany made the blood of most Americans run cold. Although very few in 1938 thought European politics were the direct

German chancellor Adolf Hitler (right) plays host to Max Schmeling in late June 1936, shortly after the German boxer knocked out Louis. Schmeling's victory was hailed throughout Nazi Germany as a triumph of Aryan supremacy.

business of the United States, there was all the same a widespread revulsion at Hitler's tyranny. As the Nazis fawned over Schmeling, his popularity plummeted. "I sailed into New York Harbor on the S.S. *Bremen* about six weeks before the fight," he recounted. "I was surprised to see the picketing. Demonstrators on shore carried signs saying 'Schmeling Go Home.' I was told 'You are just fighting for the money. You will bring the money to Hitler to build military weapons.' I received threatening letters that were often signed with 'Heil Hitler' or 'Hit Hitler.' "

As Schmeling's appeal dropped, Louis's soared. Suddenly, all that stood between Schmeling, Hitler, and the heavyweight championship was a quiet, modest young man who had been born into the grinding poverty of rural Alabama, who had dropped out of school in the sixth grade, who had worked shoving truck bodies onto a conveyer belt at the River Rouge plant of the Ford Motor Company in Dearborn,

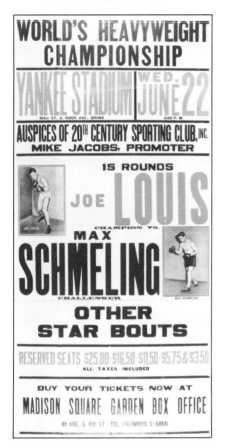

A poster advertising Louis's defense of his heavyweight title on June 22, 1938, in a rematch against Max Schmeling.

Michigan. "Now here I was a black man. I had the burden of representing all America. . . . White Americans—even while some of them were lynching black people in the South—were depending on me to K.O. Germany," he remembered.

It was a dismal irony. Had Louis not been the heavyweight champion, the restaurants and barbershops in midtown Manhattan would have denied him service because he was black. If he had wished to return to his birthplace in Alabama, he would have been forced to ride in the "colored" section of a railway car and, on his arrival, would have seen Whites Only signs at every decent public accommodation, from hotels to water fountains.

Yet not long before the big fight, President Franklin D. Roosevelt invited this "second-class citizen" to the White House, even going so far as to send a Lincoln sedan to pick him up. The president laughed and kidded with the champion, and after feeling his biceps and insisting Louis do the same to his, Roosevelt said, "Joe, we're depending on those muscles for America."

"I'm backing up America against Germany, so you know I am going to town," the champion promised. At a camp in Pompton Lakes, New Jersey, in the Ramapo Mountains 25 miles from New York City, he trained hard for the best part of a month. Before other fights, Louis liked to leave camp now and then for a round of golf. This time he wanted nothing to distract his attention, and his golf clubs stayed home.

Every day, Louis pushed himself through the grueling regimen of the boxer: roadwork (five to eight miles), hours of punching the light and heavy bags, push-ups, sit-ups, shadowboxing. He chose George Nicholson for one of his sparring partners and paid him what was then an impressive $25 a day. Nicholson earned every penny of it; he was the best there was. Twice a week, Louis boxed against Nicholson and two other fighters, going two three-minute rounds with each. They did their best to emulate Schmeling's right. "I just sparred and sparred with my partners, with them constantly throwing those right hands," Louis recalled. "Got so I could easily block them."

These sparring matches were open to the public, and on gentle spring days several thousand people made the excursion to New Jersey, paid the one-dollar admission charge to Louis's camp, refreshed themselves at the little bar on the premises, and watched Louis work out. The most vocal visitors were blacks from the Harlem district of New York City, anxious to cheer their hero. Regularly, less welcome guests turned up: American Nazis, the homegrown admirers of Hitler. Louis remembered that "they'd come to my camp day after day with swastikas on their arms. They watched me train and sat around laughing like jackasses. But it would have taken more than those fools to unnerve me at this stage."

With Jack Blackburn, his trainer, Louis studied the film of his first fight with Schmeling, caught his mistakes, and devised a new strategy. He would, literally, come out swinging. Schmeling needed a moment to plant his feet before launching his right. Louis would not give it to him. He would be the aggressor, pounding the German, backing him up, not letting him retaliate. It was the boldest strategy known to boxing, but as he broke training camp the morning of the fight, Louis was free of doubt. "I knew my body was in prime condition," he said. "I knew— I didn't think, I *knew*—I was going to beat Schmeling."

After the weigh-in at the Garden, Louis and his entourage raced uptown to a friend's apartment at 66 St. Nicholas Place in Harlem. The champion had a lunch of steak and salad, and later he took a long stroll along the Harlem River with his trainers.

"How do you feel, Joe?" asked one as they walked.

"I'm scared," the champion replied.

"Scared?"

"Yeah, I'm scared I might kill Schmeling tonight."

Around 7:00 P.M., Louis and his friends left for Yankee Stadium in the Bronx. "There were cops wherever you looked," he remembered. "When we got to the stadium, you could hardly get in. Them bluecoats were everywhere. Going up, we didn't laugh much. Nobody made jokes. It was an important fight." In his dressing room, Louis calmly stretched out on a padded table and fell asleep, leaving the anticipation and worry to his seconds.

While the champion dozed, more than 70,000 spectators flowed toward the stadium. On nearby Jerome Avenue, a group of American Communists, doing the bidding of the Soviet Union, picketed and handed out leaflets denouncing Schmeling and Hitler. Outshouting the shabby radicals, scalpers hawked tickets for ringside seats. Fight goers found themselves paying more than $100 for a ticket inside the 10th row and $85 for seats in the 10th to 15th rows.

Well-known faces were everywhere. Former heavyweight champions Jack Dempsey, Gene Tunney, Jack Sharkey, Max Baer, and James J. Braddock beamed and acknowledged cheers, some real, some imaginary. A 35-year-old man with an unusually shaped nose and a receding hairline wisecracked his way to the press section. Years earlier, when he was known as Packy East, he had fought, and lost, 21 amateur fights; now, under the name Bob Hope, he was the fastest-rising star of American comedy. Nearly everyone at ringside, from cabinet members to the working press, turned to watch socialite Evalyn Walsh McClean drift toward her seat. Around her neck, in a platinum setting, dangled the most famous gem in the world, the 44¼-carat Hope Diamond.

Louis follows through on his strategy against Max Schmeling in their rematch at New York's Yankee Stadium. By constantly following his jab with another punch, Louis was able to keep Schmeling off balance and prevent him from unleashing a solid counterpunch.

The main event was scheduled for 10:00 P.M. In the ring, under klieg lights hung from a specially constructed scaffolding, the preliminary bouts neared conclusion. They had attracted only passing attention.

At 9:00, Blackburn, always called "Chappie" by the champion, awoke Louis and started to bandage his hands. "In three rounds, Chappie," Louis said as the trainer wound white athletic tape around his palms and across his knuckles. "If I don't have Schmeling knocked out, you better come and get me, because after that, I'm through." His hands taped, he started shadowboxing. Usually, he did 10 minutes' worth, just long enough to raise a light sweat. This time, his fists drilled the air for a half hour, right until it was time to leave for the ring.

To keep his body warm, Louis put on an old flannel robe over his black-and-red trunks. For show, he draped a robe of blue silk on top. Then he came

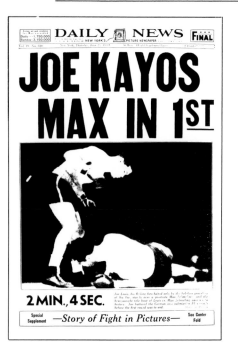

The headline tells it all: Louis knocked out Max Schmeling just 124 seconds into their championship bout.

onto the ballpark's playing field from the home team's dugout.

Outside the stadium, people on the platform at the elevated subway station overlooking the center field bleachers stood on their toes to get a glimpse of the champion. In the upper deck, in the three-dollar section under the stadium's famous scalloped facade, the laborers and clerks and maids, whose seats were as far from ringside as their plain lives were from Bob Hope's and Evalyn Walsh McClean's, cheered themselves hoarse. As Louis reached the ring, wrote a witness, "an immeasurable shout filled the ballpark, the kind the stadium had first heard years ago when Babe Ruth rode one out during a World Series."

Next, from the visiting team's dugout, strode Schmeling, encircled by 20 New York City policemen. He had on the same gray bathrobe he had worn for the 1936 fight. As he came into sight, a few people offered polite applause. But they were drowned out by jeers. "As I walked down the long path to the ring," Schmeling remembered nearly a half century later, "I put a towel over my head to protect myself from the cigarette boxes, banana peels, and paper cups that were thrown at me." The police climbed through the ropes of the ring with him, aiming to block anything else that might be hurled.

In their respective corners, the fighters slipped on their boxing gloves. Ring announcer Harry Balogh hurried through the obligatory introductions of some boxing has-beens. In the first row, broadcaster Clem McCarthy rasped an account of the preliminaries into an NBC microphone. Seventy million listeners from coast to coast heard him predict "the greatest fight of our generation." A few yards away, Arno Helmers, the official Nazi broadcaster, droned on, his gruff, clipped voice carried by the shortwave to Germany, where at three in the morning millions of Schmeling's countrymen were by their radios. At Berchtesgaden, Hitler listened while he paced back and forth.

Balogh bellowed an introduction of Schmeling—"the outstanding contender"—and Louis—"the famous Detroit Brown Bomber." The police, the promoters, the managers started climbing through the ropes out of the ring. Referee Arthur Donovan motioned the fighters toward him for instructions. "I don't want anybody from your corners sticking his head through the ropes during this fight," he warned. "It may cause serious trouble." The referee then asked them to give the crowd "the greatest fight in heavyweight history" and sent them back to their corners.

The stadium throng hushed, waiting for the bell. Schmeling stood still, arms at his side, staring at Louis and listening to some last-second advice from his trainer. In his corner 25 feet away, the champion kept moving, dancing lightly up and down, his body glistening with sweat.

The bell sounded, the crowd roared, and, bobbing their heads, the fighters met in the center of the ring. Schmeling, his face unshaven, grinned confidently. Then Louis hit him, and he stopped smiling. It was a jab, and it made the German's greased hair fly up from his head. It was the first blow of what Grantland Rice, the dean of American sportswriters, called "the most savage and sensational attack ever seen in a ring." Schmeling brushed his right glove across his forehead. Showing not the slightest expression, Louis bore into him with a series of rights and lefts that backed the challenger into the ropes.

None of the punches traveled more than eight inches, but as another fighter once said, the champion's short jab felt "like a bomb bursting in your face." Schmeling fired his first punch of the evening, his vaunted right, but it was harmless. Against the ropes he was a sitting duck, and Louis pummeled him with shots to the head and body. "Move, Max, move!" yelled his trainer. But Schmeling stayed planted, trying to ward off the barrage with weak jabs, finding an instant's relief by falling into a clinch.

Now Louis was throwing longer punches. An overhand right, swung from the shoulder, slammed into Schmeling's face, and he staggered backward, the ropes keeping him from falling. From then on, the German boxer remembered, "the fight was a complete haze for me." Louis threw a long right just as Schmeling was turning, causing the blow to land on the side of his back. At ringside, they heard Schmeling "scream like a frightened girl or a stuck pig."

"Geez, it scared me because I never heard anything like that before," Donovan said later. The punch had shattered two of Schmeling's vertebrae. His mouth hung open, but Louis promptly closed it with an assault to the head.

When Schmeling grabbed the top rope with both hands, Donovan stepped in. The referee backed Louis off and started a standing-eight count, but Schmeling moved away at the count of two and lurched toward the center of the ring. He could not raise his left arm.

Seventy thousand people were standing, shrieking, shaking the stadium to its foundations. Louis barreled in with a left and followed it with a wicked right that landed flush on the jaw. Schmeling toppled forward and rolled onto his back. Donovan headed Louis to a neutral corner, but Schmeling heaved himself up. On legs giving the barest of support, with no sense of direction or coordination, he assumed a pathetic imitation of his stance and gamely, instinctively, pressed on.

Louis caught him with a left hook and a right cross that sent Schmeling back to his hands and knees. Once more he got up, his face the color of a steamed clam. Donovan wiped resin off the challenger's gloves. Louis bounced up and down, anxious for the referee to get out of his way.

On NBC radio, Clem McCarthy described what happened next: "A left to the head, a left to the jaw,

Louis in his dressing room at Yankee Stadium, right after he defeated Max Schmeling. In eulogizing Louis at his funeral years later, civil rights leader Jesse Jackson said of the boxer's monumental victory, "Usually the champion rides on the shoulder of the nation and its people, but in this case, the nation rode on the shoulders of the hero."

a right to the head and Donovan is watching carefully. Right to the body, a left hook to the jaw, and Schmeling is down." From his corner, a white towel flew into the ring, nearly hitting Donovan in the face. The traditional sign of boxing surrender was unrecognized by New York's rules, so Donovan tossed it back. It landed on the center rope, neatly folded.

The referee stood over Schmeling, counting to 10. "The count is five. . . . Five . . . six . . . seven . . . eight . . ." McCarthy was saying. The sportswriter Stanley Woodward saw Schmeling on his hands and knees. The former champion, Woodward said, "looked vaguely around with a helpless silly look in his eyes. He was beaten. He might have got up, but he would have been killed."

Donovan got no further than eight. He waved his hands and stopped the fight.

Men poured into the ring. Louis gave a small smile. A microphone dropped down from the scaffolding, and Balogh cried into it: "The time two minutes, four seconds, first round. Referee stops it. The winner and still champion, Joe Louis."

2

"MAN, THROW THAT VIOLIN AWAY!"

The FUTURE HEAVYWEIGHT champion of the world was born on May 13, 1914, in a creaking, unpainted sharecropper's cabin not far from the small town of Lafayette, Alabama. He was named Joe Louis Barrow, and during his youth that is how he was known, dropping the "Barrow" only when he became a boxer.

Munroe Barrow, his father, was a strapping man, 6 feet 4 inches and 200 pounds, who spent most of his life as a sharecropper trying to scratch a living out of the red clay soil of Alabama. The son of a slave, he rented a 120-acre farm several years before Joe's birth and had dreams of making it pay. Before long, his hopes were ruined. The endless days of picking cotton to make the barest of livings proved too much for him, and Munroe Barrow lost his emotional stability. When Joe was two, his father was committed to the Searcy State Hospital for the Colored Insane. "He died there when he was 58 years old," his son said. "He never knew I was champion."

The prospects for the Barrow family could scarcely have been more dismal. Munroe left for his wife, Lillie, a small mountain of debts and a run-down rented farm with a drafty, ramshackle cabin. Against stiff odds, Lillie Reese Barrow held together her brood of eight children. During the next few years, she moved the family from one rented farm to another, making a crop at each place. "She worked as hard,

Louis's father, Munroe Barrow, poses with four of Joe's seven siblings a few years before the fighter was born. When Joe was two years old, his father was found to be emotionally disturbed and was committed to an Alabama state hospital, where he remained for the rest of his life.

and many times harder, than any man around," Joe said of his mother. "She could plow a good straight furrow, plant and pick with the best of them—cut cord wood like a lumberjack then leave the fields an hour earlier than anyone else and fix a meal to serve to her family."

As an infant, Joe seemed to cry every waking moment. "Joe could holler loud as a wildcat," remembered a relative. As Joe got older, he craved his mother's approval. "When I was just a little boy, I always wanted my momma to smile on me," he said. Now and then, he would sneak off to avoid a household chore, but more often, and without being asked, he would get down on his hands and knees and scrub the cabin's floors. When Lillie, dead tired from working in the fields, would see the spotless floor and her son beaming from ear to ear, "she'd grab me and give me a big kiss for it. Then I could have floated clear up to the sky."

Just as surely as a good deed was rewarded with a hug and a kiss, misbehavior led to a whipping. One time, Lillie fixed a big lunch and gave Joe precise instructions to deliver it at noon to the field where she and everyone else would be working. Joe waited all morning, going outside every few minutes to check the sun's position. When the sun was right overhead, he grabbed the basket and started toward the field. He then made the mistake of lifting the basket's lid. The first thing he spied was a baked chicken leg. By the time he got to the field, the basket was half empty. For the rest of the day, Joe found it rather painful to sit down. "I cried some mean tears," he said of the thrashing, "but my stomach was happy."

Lillie did not always punish her little boy with a spanking. Once, Joe came across part of a bottle of moonshine, a particularly potent, illegally distilled liquor. Naturally, he drank it, and naturally he got drunk, eventually passing out under a tree. When he

sobered up, he felt the sting not of a switch but of his mother's tongue. She gave him a bitter lecture on the evils of drink, and it was not until middle age that he drank again.

Even though the Barrows were poor, no one went hungry, and for Joe the Alabama countryside held nearly all a little boy could wish. Too small to be of any use picking cotton, he was on his own when the others left home for the fields each day at dawn. He loved exploring the woods and swimming and fishing at a nearby pond. In the evenings, with his sister Eulalia, he played the dangerous game of fireball. "You make a ball out of rags," Eulalia explained, "tie it with a string, soak it in kerosene, light it and throw it to each other. You had to be quick to get rid of it before it'd burn you."

On Sundays, Lillie outfitted her children in their best clothes—for Joe that meant a clean pair of overalls—and led them to the Mt. Sinai Baptist Church.

Louis was born in this sharecropper's shack on a rented farm near Lafayette, Alabama.

Devoutly religious, Joe's mother insisted that her children keep their faith. Whatever the weather, however rutted the roads, the Barrows made it to the spirited, daylong services at Mt. Sinai.

Sometime during this period, Lillie was told (falsely, as it turned out) that Munroe had died in the asylum. Believing that her husband was dead, she agreed to marry Pat Brooks, a local widower. Left with eight children, Brooks did not seem to mind marrying a woman with eight of her own. "Anyone who would marry a lady with so many kids had to be a nice man," observed a relative.

Too big for the Barrow place, the enormous combined family squeezed into Brooks's house in nearby

When Louis was still very young, his mother, Lillie Reese Barrow, got remarried, to Pat Brooks, a local widower with eight children. Their huge combined family lived in a small wooden house in eastern Alabama for several years.

Camp Hill. Joe quickly developed a fondness for his new stepfather, a former sharecropper who had found better-paying work with a bridge construction firm. "He was always fair and treated all those sixteen children as equally as a man could," Joe recalled.

For the Barrows, Camp Hill was a step up. Brooks's house had an organ, rugs on the floors, and, best of all, a Model T Ford parked outside. "Every Sunday, all of us would pile into that old car and go to church," Joe's youngest sister recalled. "There were no paved streets, lots of large holes and ditches in the road. We were lucky not to break an axle every time we went."

From October through April, the Mt. Sinai Church operated a school for the black children of the area. Joe attended and hated it. Part of the problem was a slight speech impediment that made recitation embarrassing and caused him to clam up. "I stammered and stuttered, and I guess I was so plain nervous that the other kids laughed at me," he recalled. Rather than suffer the taunts of his schoolmates, Joe started wandering away from the classroom to be by himself. "Why should I stay in school and be made fun of," he wondered, "when there were snakes to catch or a cool spot under a shady tree where I could watch the clouds change shape?"

As a boy, Joe was never slapped in the face by racial prejudice. He played with neighboring white children and never heard any of them call him "nigger." That demeaning word had been heard often enough by his mother and stepfather, yet they were spared the racial violence employed by the Ku Klux Klan and other white supremacist groups in the South to keep blacks "in their place." In fact, Pat and Lillie Brooks were driving home in the Model T late one night when a contingent of Klansmen, hooded and masked in white robes, suddenly waved their car to a stop. The Klan closed in, intent on punishing some black for a crime, real or imagined. As they were about to yank Joe's stepfather from the car, a voice piped up: "That's Pat Brooks. He's a *good* nigger." The Klansmen let them go.

Being a "good nigger" was the way to survive. A "good nigger" let whites call him "boy." He stepped aside when a white person approached on a sidewalk. He always went to the back door of a white's house, and when his knock was answered, he put his hat in his hands, cast his eyes downward, and spoke only when spoken to. He farmed the poorest land, got the worst-paying job, and was the first to be laid off and the last to be hired back.

By 1926, Pat Brooks had his fill of being a "good nigger." Two of his brothers had moved north, from Alabama to Detroit, and they brought back stories of better things. It was not a paradise they described, but jobs with the automobile factories were easy to come by, wages were good, and blacks got a fairer deal than in the South. Shortly after the frightening encounter with the Klan, Brooks made up his mind to move to Detroit. Leaving his family behind, he headed north, aiming to find a job, settle in, and then send for all the Brookses and Barrows.

Brooks was following a well-worn path. Around the turn of the century, southern blacks, sick of poverty and discrimination, started pulling up stakes and moving away to assume industrial jobs in northern cities and towns. By the 1920s, their most common destination was Detroit. In 1910, only 5,741 blacks lived there; by 1930, the black population numbered 125,000, nearly all recent arrivals from the South. Blacks, of course, were not the only ones flocking to the city. Immigrants from Europe and farm families from the East and Midwest also arrived in great numbers. When Pat Brooks climbed off the train from Alabama in 1926, he was setting foot in the country's fourth largest city; nearly 1 million people called it home.

Detroit grew because it built cars, and in the 1920s it could not build them fast enough. Dodge, Olds, Buick, Packard, and a hundred other firms clamored for workers to man their assembly lines. But for virtually every Detroit newcomer, white or black, the magic name was neither Dodge nor Buick. It was Ford. In 1914, Henry Ford had astounded the industrial world by offering a daily wage of five dollars to the workers assembling his Model T. A good two dollars above the going wage, the five-dollar day was more than most workers had dreamed of. In addition, Ford did not discriminate against blacks. By 1926, the company employed 10,000 blacks, many as supervisors and foremen.

At first, Brooks was not lucky enough to find work at Ford. His initial job was sweeping streets for the city. But he kept trying and eventually landed one of the coveted assembly-line positions at Ford's River Rouge plant, the largest factory in the world. In the meantime, he sent for the rest of his family.

Twelve-year-old Joe took the big move in stride. The months of hearing his elders talk about the wonders of Detroit had spoiled for him the simple pleasures of Alabama, and he could not wait to leave. Detroit did not disappoint him in the slightest. "I never saw so many people in one place," he said later, "so many cars at one time; I had never even seen a trolley before." The city slickers in their fine clothes made him, in his overalls and country shoes, feel more than a little out of place, but he would get the right outfits in no time. All in all, he remembered, "Detroit looked awfully good to me."

After briefly doubling up with some relatives, the Barrows and Brookses found a home of their own, a rambling eight-room tenement on Detroit's East Side. Joe, now wearing sweaters and knickers, was enrolled in the Duffield Elementary School. As in Alabama, he had a hard time of it. His education at Mt. Sinai had been spotty, putting him years behind the children in Detroit, so at Duffield he was assigned to the third grade. Twelve years old and large for his age, Joe dwarfed his younger classmates. Embarrassed by his stutter and unfamiliar with the ways of a northern city school, he kept his mouth closed and during lessons spent his time gazing out the window, imagining himself somewhere else—anywhere else.

For three years, Joe struggled along, finally making it into the sixth grade. His teacher told him he would get no further and pushed him into vocational training. "He's going to have to make a living with his hands," said one teacher. "He'd better start now." Transferring to the Bronson Trade School, Joe did well in carpentry and cabinetmaking, turning out shelves, tables, and chairs. "When I finished them off, I took them home to be used in the house," he said. "It helped. Furniture was the last thing we needed to buy."

By the early 1930s, the family needed all the help it could get. The Great Depression hit Detroit hard. When auto sales plummeted, Ford and the other firms started laying off their employees, and Joe's stepfather and several of his older brothers lost their jobs. The shining promise of Detroit was revealed to be fool's gold. During hard times in Alabama, there had always been, at the very least, enough to eat. In Detroit, it was different. "We was always hungry," recalled Lillie. "Joe didn't even have shoes to put on when he went to school." Desperate, the family turned to charity and public assistance, waiting in long, dreary lines for free meals in soup kitchens and accepting a meager relief check of a few dollars a week.

Joe did what he could. Nearly every morning, he hurried to the Eastern Market, where he was paid 50 cents for unpacking fruit and arranging it for sale. In the afternoons, he and his close friend Freddie Guinyard made deliveries for a local ice company. Driving

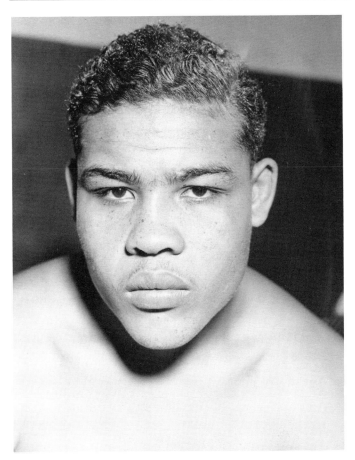

Louis's determination to win the heavyweight title is captured in this photograph, taken when he was in his early twenties. His subsequent success in boxing prompted militant black leader Malcolm X to say of him, "Every Negro boy old enough to walk wanted to be the next Brown Bomber."

a horse-drawn wagon all over Detroit, Joe earned one dollar a day. Freddie, barely 100 pounds and unable to heft as much as Joe, got 50 cents and during most deliveries minded the horse while Joe lugged 60-pound blocks of ice up flights of stairs to waiting customers.

Not every moment was spent working or at trade school. During these years, Joe kept steady company with Bonnie Franklin, the stepdaughter of one of his older sisters. He visited her whenever he could, and the two often sneaked off to the movies. He also had time to flirt with trouble, hanging around with a local street gang whose members liked to steal fruit and taunt the police. "We had fights, but nothing much,"

Joe recalled. "Just gang fights the way kids do. You got into a fight and you punched the best you could."

Worried about her son, Lillie attempted to point him toward culture, somehow scraping together the money for violin lessons. Joe dutifully studied notes and scales and gamely sawed away at the violin's strings with his bow. He showed not the smallest aptitude for the instrument. By now he was a hulking six-footer, and the sight of this young giant carrying a delicate violin with him to trade school amused his classmates. Joe dealt with their mirth directly: "I remember one time some guy called me a sissy when he saw me with the violin, and I broke it over his head."

Thurston McKinney, a fellow trade school student, found Joe's violin as funny as everyone else did, but he did not cry "Sissy!" Instead, he asked Joe to come to the gym with him. An accomplished amateur boxer (he was a 1932 Detroit Golden Gloves champion), McKinney trained at the Brewster Recreation Center. Joe liked the place instantly. Before long, he was spending all his spare time there, using the 50 cents his mother had given him for violin lessons to rent a locker.

When Thurston asked Joe one day to be his sparring partner, he happily accepted. After being knocked about for a round or two, Joe lost his temper, let loose with his right hand, and caught Thurston squarely on the jaw, nearly knocking out the Golden Gloves champion. Thurston shook his head, grinned at Joe, and said, "Man, throw that violin away!"

Having felt Joe's punch, Thurston went to work, tirelessly promoting what boxing had to offer. He opened a copy of *Ring* magazine, boxing's bible, and pointed to an account of how many millions Jack Dempsey, the heavyweight champion of the 1920s, had made in the ring. Even an amateur fighter, Thurston said, could come away from a bout with a check worth $7 to $25 in merchandise. "He worked on me like that and the idea of big money kind of swelled in my head," Joe recalled.

In short order, he abandoned both the violin and trade school. He missed neither, because now, he explained, "I could say out loud, 'I'm going to be a fighter. I'm going to be somebody.' It gave me a sense of pride and dignity to at last want to be something." Reluctantly, his mother gave him her blessing.

Joe's family was still hard up and could not afford to have him spending all his time at the gym. So he found work. For eight hours a day at the Briggs Motor Company, he pushed truck bodies to the paint sprayer on the assembly line. At five each evening, he left the factory, raced home for dinner, and then, as soon as he could, he went to the gym. ✺

3

"YOU GOTTA KNOCK 'EM OUT"

BOXING IS THE most physical, most direct of sports. Its object is the simplest in the world: Hit your opponent and keep him from hitting you. Its fundamentals are swiftly learned. There is a basic stance, several basic punches—the straight blow, the hook, the jab, the uppercut, the cross—and a few basic defensive moves: clinching, parrying, slipping a punch, covering up, and, most instinctively, ducking. Yet advancing from novice to champion is perhaps the most difficult thing in sports, demanding of the fighter speed—both of the hands and of the feet—strength, stamina, an almost impossible fitness, a cool head, and, above all else, courage.

For 20 years, Joe Louis Barrow demonstrated a possession of every quality save foot speed. In 1932, however, he demonstrated only untamed athletic talent and a mean right hand. "Punch. I could punch you and knock you out," he said of those days, "if I could catch you." He trained at nights and on weekends at the Brewster Recreation Center on Detroit's East Side, trying to master the fundamentals, doing what the boxing instructors told him.

After so much practice, he was hungry for a fight. Filling out a fight application form, writing with a large, bold script, he got only "Joe Louis" written before running out of space. "Don't worry about the 'Barrow,' " he was told. " 'Joe Louis' will be enough."

Lillie Reese Barrow offers her son a bit of motherly advice. Throughout Louis's boxing career, his managers and handlers publicized him as he appears here: polite and dutiful.

39

Not long afterward, his sister sewed for him a shiny jacket with the name *Joe Louis* embroidered on the back. He wore the jacket everywhere, and the shortened name became his own.

Before his first fight, Joe Louis was the picture of confidence. He had studied a photograph of his opponent, a light heavyweight named Johnny Miler, and saw a fighter he knew he could beat. Holman Williams, the trainer at the Brewster Center, cautioned him that Miler had experience; he had boxed for the United States at the 1932 Olympics in Los Angeles. Louis ignored the warning and invited his friends along to share in his inevitable triumph.

In the first two rounds, Miler knocked Louis down seven times. "Joe's face was all skinned up," remembered a witness. "He took a bad whipping." For his sorry effort, Louis was handed a merchandise check worth seven dollars. At home, seeing her son battered and bruised, his mother burst into tears and told him he had better find something else to do. The next day, his stepfather suggested much the same thing, counseling him to settle down with a regular job and a nice girl.

For a while, Louis took their advice. Changing jobs, he went to work at Ford, where for eight hours a day he shoved truck bodies onto a conveyor belt. He made $25 a week. For several months, he steered clear of the gym, but the backbreaking job at Ford took its toll: "I figured, if I'm going to hurt that much for $25 a week, I might as well go back and try fighting again."

Knowing what it meant to be knocked from pillar to post, Louis trained with a new dedication. The people at Brewster welcomed him back with open arms and began scheduling fights he stood a chance of winning. His second amateur bout was more like it. He dispatched his hapless opponent with two punches, a left hook followed by a straight right to the jaw. It was his first knockout, and he was on top of the world. He stayed there for a time, winning his next 13 fights, all by knockouts, collecting $25 gift certificates for each.

The reward for this success was a move to the sterner competition of the Golden Gloves and Amateur Athletic Union (AAU) tournaments. The Golden Gloves and AAU staged their matches all over, and Louis fought in Chicago, Boston, and Toronto. Away from his family for the first time, he was not homesick for long, as he quickly learned to like the company of his fellow fighters. "You knew all the guys in the amateur circle, you'd eat and sleep together, and you became friends," he said. And they liked him. Still very quiet—the result of his lifelong speech impediment—he was, all the same, one of the guys. "Every night, we'd tease him. . . . He'd laugh more at the jokes we'd tell on him than we did," said a friend. "But when he got in the ring, he had that deadpan look and that followed him through his whole career."

Of 54 amateur bouts, Louis won 50, 43 by knockout. He got in trouble only when he faced more experienced foes. In the 1933 AAU national championship for light heavyweights, which was held in Boston, he lost to Max Marek, a former Notre Dame football star and a seasoned fighter. Marek did not hurt Louis but skillfully parried his punches. The judges awarded Marek the decision, and for years he cashed in on his victory by running a bar and grill in Chicago with a big sign out front inviting customers to come in, buy a drink, and shake hands with the Man Who Beat Joe Louis.

Louis also met his match in Stanley Evans, another light heavyweight from Detroit. In preparing for their bout, Evans did the right thing. "I had watched him train and I knew if he hit you, you were down," he said. So Evans employed a defensive strat-

Louis (second from right) poses with a group of Chicago Golden Gloves boxers in early 1934. He joined the professional ranks that same year, a few months after his 20th birthday.

egy, blocking Louis's punches, then swiftly counter-punching. He did not come close to a knockout, but he won the three-round fight by decision. Early in 1934, Louis got his revenge. He beat Evans decisively in a rematch, winning the Detroit Golden Gloves title in the process.

In his dressing room one night following a victory, Louis was introduced to a heavyset black man who wore a gray silk suit and conducted himself in the refined way of a gentleman. His name was John Roxborough, and after congratulating Louis he invited him to stop by his real estate office in a day or two for a little talk.

Roxborough was a pillar of Detroit's black community. Coming from a respected family—his brother was a state senator, his nephew a diplomat—Roxborough had interests in real estate and insurance, and he regularly patronized black charities and civic organizations. The source of his wealth and influence, however, was neither business nor philanthropy but gambling. He was the acknowledged king of the Detroit numbers racket, which penetrated every black neighborhood. Unable to afford racetracks and private casinos, blacks in big cities played a less costly game. The player chose a three-digit number, bet a penny or two on it, and if that number turned up in the next day's stock market listings or pari-mutuel totals at a racetrack, he or she won. Irresistible as it was illegal, the numbers involved millions of dollars, and Roxborough was its majordomo in Detroit, overseeing the collection of bets, paying off the lucky winners, and, naturally, keeping a tidy profit for himself.

A fine basketball player in his youth, Roxborough carefully followed athletics in black Detroit, frequently reaching into his pocket to finance amateur teams. Thurston McKinney, Louis's partner from the Brewster Center, appealed to Roxborough on his friend's behalf. "Mr. Roxborough," he said, "there's a sweet-looking amateur you might want to look at. He could sure use some help. He doesn't even own a pair of trunks. But can he punch."

Roxborough's ears perked up. He was used to lending a helping hand. Furthermore, if this Louis was really as good as people said—of championship caliber—the person managing his career stood to make a fortune. Roxborough meant to be that man.

During their pleasant conversation in the real estate office, Roxborough decided to back the young fighter. He escorted Louis to a pharmacy, then to a sporting goods store, telling the owner at each place to give the boy anything he needed. For the first time, Louis had all the proper tools of his trade: professional gloves, trunks, shoes, tape, and bandages. Seeing his worn-out clothes, Roxborough gave him his own old suits and shirts, having the sleeves and trousers lengthened. He insisted that Louis eat a heavyweight's diet and made him give up frankfurters and ice cream for the protein of steak and the carbohydrates of potatoes.

For a time, Louis virtually lived with the Roxboroughs. "It was a beautiful house, and he had a good looking and gracious wife," he said. "I loved it. I never saw black people living this way, and I was envious and watched everything he did."

With Roxborough paying the bills, Louis devoted himself to boxing and fell into a regular training schedule. As he won fight after fight, it became obvious that his days as an amateur were numbered. Whenever he collected a $25 gift certificate for a victory, he could not help but imagine himself accepting one of the giant purses of the professional ranks.

In April 1934, Louis won the AAU light-heavyweight title. Two months later, after knocking out a light heavyweight from Cleveland in the first round, he told Roxborough he was ready to turn pro. "I tried to talk Joe out of it," Roxborough said years later. The older man asked Louis what the rush was, suggesting that the 20 year old might not be ready. But it was actually Roxborough himself who was not ready. In the midst of a divorce, he was strapped for cash and, for all his savvy, was more than a little unsure of himself in the world of professional boxing.

Louis would not be put off. "Mr. Roxborough, I want the money," he said.

"That I could understand," Roxborough recalled. "That was why I was in the numbers business—and I've never been ashamed of it—and I said 'O.K. Joe. I'll find you a good manager and a good trainer.' "

He turned to his friend Julian Black of Chicago. A stocky black man with slicked-back hair, a slight limp, and a brusque manner, Black was a major operator in the Chicago numbers. More to the point, he had managed professional fighters before, and he knew his way where Roxborough did not. When Roxborough described the great promise of the heavyweight he had in Detroit, Black gladly agreed to

become a comanager. He told Roxborough to bring his fighter to Chicago, where Black would set him up with a place to live and a place to train.

At the railroad station a few days later, Black greeted Roxborough with a smile and Louis with a long, hard look. Wasting few words, Black told Louis that his first professional fight would be in a month, and he had better start training hard.

After showing Louis to his Chicago home—a room in an apartment near Washington Park—Roxborough and Black dropped in at George Trafton's gym on Randolph Street. There they found who they were looking for: Jack Blackburn, a friend of Black's and a well-regarded trainer. Years earlier, Blackburn had been a hard-as-nails lightweight fighter. But black boxers seldom got shots at championships, and his career had stalled a long way from the top. He

Louis with (from left to right) his handler, Julian Black; trainer, Jack Blackburn; manager, John Roxborough; and instructor, Russell Cowans. Eager for the fighter to maintain a positive public image, Black and Roxborough hired Cowans, a sportswriter and college graduate, to tutor Louis in the basics of history, grammar, and arithmetic.

was also his own worst enemy. An alcoholic, he occasionally became uncontrollably violent when drunk, once murdering a man in a Philadelphia bar fight and serving time in prison for the crime. Now 50, balding, with a jagged scar on the left side of his face—the reminder of a long-ago knife fight—Blackburn was working at Trafton's, training several mediocre fighters, all of them white.

As Black and Roxborough sang the praises of their young man, Blackburn's interest grew. There was one thing he needed to know. "What is this Louis?" he asked. "A white boy?"

"No. He's a colored boy who can bat a thousand in any league," Roxborough replied.

Blackburn shook his head. "No sireee," he said. "Not for me. You can't make no good money with a colored boy. He won't have no chance. You can count me right out."

At that moment, though, Blackburn was not making any money to speak of with his white fighters. So, when Roxborough offered him a generous $35 a week to train Louis, he agreed.

The next day, Blackburn saw his new charge for the first time. The trainer was not particularly impressed. At 6 feet, Louis was tall enough, but at 175 pounds he was too thin for a heavyweight. When he got into the ring, it pained Blackburn to watch. For sure, he had powerful hands, and they were extremely fast, but his footwork was slow, he showed little in the way of defense, he could not throw a combination of punches, and he was continually off balance. Yet there was no denying his strength or his quick reflexes. Most important of all, Blackburn took an instant liking to the young man with the quiet manner.

The trainer placed Louis on a demanding regimen: up each morning before dawn for a run of six miles in Washington Park, an enormous breakfast, some rest, then every afternoon a workout at Trafton's. During the first week, Blackburn did not allow Louis in the ring. Hour after hour, he made Louis hit the heavy bag, demanding he throw punches with his feet planted firmly so as not to be thrown off balance. Lead with your left, Blackburn instructed, then follow with the right.

After a week, he and Louis got into the ring together. Still agile at 50, Blackburn threw punch after punch.

"I had to block it," Louis recalled. "I wasn't allowed to duck. When he threw a right hand, I had to catch it and he told me that any time somebody missed, you should hit him. He taught that if you can throw one punch, you can throw two, you can throw three because you're always on balance."

During a break one afternoon, Blackburn told Louis what he was up against. "You know, boy, the

Louis prepares for his August 1935 heavyweight match against King Levinsky by sparring with Willie Davis. In his second bout as a professional, Louis had knocked out Davis to garner a modest $62 prize.

heavyweight division for a Negro is hardly likely," he said. "The white man ain't too keen on it. You have to be really something to get somewhere."

With each passing day, Blackburn saw that Louis was going to be "really something." He was a quick learner who scarcely resembled the awkward bruiser Blackburn had watched in the ring a few weeks before. "You got to listen to everything I tell you," he said to his fighter. "You got to jump when I say jump, sleep when I say sleep. Other than that you're wasting my time." Louis looked him in the eye and promised there would be no wasted time.

"OK, Chappie," replied Blackburn, allowing himself a small, tight smile.

Louis's face broke into a grin of its own. He said, "OK, Chappie." From then on, they were very special friends and always called one another "Chappie."

As the day of Louis's professional debut approached, Blackburn worried that the shy, calm fighter might lack the killer instinct, the controlled anger a boxer needs to pursue the knockout of an opponent. Black fighters had to have knockouts, he explained, because white judges seldom awarded them victories by decisions. "You gotta knock 'em out and keep knocking 'em out to get anywheres," he said. "Let your right fist be your referee. Don't ever forget that. Let that right fist there be your referee!"

On July 4, 1934, Louis put Blackburn's concerns to rest. At the Bacon Casino in Chicago, he fought for the first time as a professional, facing Jack Kracken, a local white heavyweight. Less than 2 minutes into the first round, using a left hook, he knocked out Kracken and won a purse of $59. Roxborough and Black, passing up their share, let Louis keep it all.

A week later, again at the Bacon Casino, Louis knocked out Willie Davis, a black heavyweight, and collected a little larger purse, $62. In the weeks that followed, Louis kept fighting and kept winning. By the end of August, his record was 5–0, with 4 knock-outs.

In September, Louis returned to Detroit for a bout with a Canadian heavyweight, Alex Borchuk. Word of Louis's success in Chicago was all over town, and his family, friends, and neighbors were in the crowd that jammed the Naval Armory. "They never knew how close I came to losing," he said years later. In the third round, Borchuk landed a punch on Louis's jaw that broke a molar. The pain was so excruciating that between rounds Louis nearly quit. But Black-burn would not let him. He told Louis what to look for, and in the fourth Louis sent Borchuk to the canvas. With his winnings, he treated his family to some new clothes and his friends to a night at the bowling alley. ❧

4

THE BROWN
BOMBER

JOE LOUIS WAS most times the soul of politeness. But one day, while he was champion, his manners failed him. At his New Jersey training camp, he caught sight of a towering, middle-aged black man with a glistening shaved head and a smile that revealed a row of gold teeth. "Get that black cat out of here," Louis muttered. "I don't want him in my camp." The man Louis wanted no part of was the former heavyweight champion of the world, Jack Johnson.

The titleholder from 1908 until 1915, Jack Johnson had been white America's worst nightmare, flaunting every convention that called upon a black to know his place. A magnificent fighter, he pummeled every white he faced and relished doing it, taunting and laughing at his fallen foes. He spent his winnings on racing cars and jewelry, in saloons and brothels, and lavished attention on white women. As he once explained, some failed romances "led me to forswear colored women and to determine that my lot henceforth would be cast only with white women." Traveling from city to city with an entourage of several white prostitutes, he put them up in separate rooms of the same hotel and, during the night, paid visits to one after another.

"It is my duty to win the championship," Louis said, "and prove to the world that, black or white, a man can become the best fighter and still be a gentleman."

One reporter characterized Johnson as the "vilest, most despicable creature that lives," and few whites disagreed. But because no white could lick him, he stayed heavyweight champion.

51

The first black to become the world heavyweight champion, Jack Johnson was clearly not the world's greatest sportsman: He liked to taunt his opponents in the ring and boast about himself everywhere else. "Don't be another Jack Johnson," Louis was constantly advised by his handlers as he worked his way toward a shot at the title.

Finally, on April 5, 1915, in Havana, Cuba, in the 26th round of a fight that might have been fixed, Johnson lost his title to Jess Willard. A seasoned vaudeville performer, Willard was at best a journeyman fighter. But he was white, and because of that he was a hero. When he returned from Cuba with the championship, his train pulled into New York in the middle of the night. Despite the late hour, thousands pressed into Pennsylvania Station, and an even larger throng cheered "the great white hope" as he proceeded to his hotel.

Having got the championship back, the white men who promoted boxing vowed never to permit another horror like Jack Johnson to contend for the title. In practice, that meant barring all blacks from championship fights. Two decades after Willard's victory, the color line was still intact, but in the lower ranks of the sport, there were more black boxers than ever before, and in nonchampionship bouts a black fighting a white was fairly common. A truly exceptional fighter who stirred the fewest memories of Johnson might, just might, have a shot at the top. Or, as Jack Blackburn told Louis during their days together at Trafton's, "If you really ain't gonna be another Jack Johnson, you got some hope. White man hasn't forgotten that fool nigger with his white women, acting like he owned the world."

Don't be another Jack Johnson. Don't be another Jack Johnson. Louis could hear it in his sleep. His retiring nature placed him as far from Johnson's flamboyance as could be imagined, but his managers and trainer took no chances. "To be a champion you've got to be a gentleman first," John Roxborough lectured Louis. "Your toughest fight might not be in the ring but out in public. We never, never say anything bad about an opponent. Before a fight you say how great you think he is; after a fight you say how great you think he was. And for God's sake, after you beat a white opponent, don't smile."

"That's what Jack Johnson did," Julian Black said.

"Joe, you're going to get a lot of invitations to nightclubs," Roxborough continued. "But you never go into one alone. And above all, you never have your picture taken with a white woman."

"There's one more thing," Blackburn said. "You never, never lose a fight."

Louis followed their advice, most notably Blackburn's. In late 1934, he fought twice at the cavernous Chicago Stadium against solid opposition. In the first fight, he knocked out Charlie Massera in the third round. The second bout was more difficult. Up against Lee Ramage, a fine defensive boxer and genuine contender for heavyweight honors, Louis struggled to find an opening. Between rounds, Blackburn told him to stop aiming for Ramage's head and stomach and go for his arms. The steady pounding paid off. By the eighth round, Ramage was having trouble holding his arms up, and when he dropped his guard an inch or two, it was all over. Louis struck with blazing speed, trapping him against the ropes and knocking him out.

Louis pocketed his share of the $2,750 purse and returned to Detroit for the Christmas holidays. In the black neighborhoods on the East Side, it was only a matter of time, everyone said, before he was the heavyweight champion. Basking in all the attention, Louis did not think twice about sharing his success with others. He bought toys for the children at his old elementary school. He gave clothes and wristwatches to all the Brookses and Barrows. And to the city of Detroit, he wrote a check for $270, repayment for the relief Pat Brooks had accepted when he had been out of work.

Louis cut quite a figure. Wearing sharp new clothes—he favored chalk-striped double-breasted suits and light-colored, broad-brimmed felt hats—he cruised by behind the wheel of his first car, a black Buick riding on tires with the widest whitewalls they made. With his pals Freddie Guinyard and Thurston McKinney, he drove the big Buick around the old neighborhood for hours. The three of them smiled at the prettiest girls, inviting them to come for a ride. "I better not see you get in Joe Louis Barrow's car," mothers started warning their daughters.

However satisfying the black Buick and his hometown celebrity were, Louis was miles from the heavyweight title. He had proved himself in Detroit and Chicago, but championships and the big money were in New York. "Yeah, he's ready for New York," Blackburn said, "but New York ain't ready for him."

New York meant Madison Square Garden and Jimmy Johnston, "the Boy Bandit," the Garden's director of boxing and the most important figure in the sport. For years, the Garden had virtually owned championship boxing. Johnston had a contract with nearly every highly ranked fighter, and he decided on, scheduled, and promoted the matches that led to championships.

By early 1935, Johnston knew about Louis and his gaudy knockout record. Faced with a serious shortage of heavyweight talent, the promoter gave John Roxborough a call. "I can help your boy," Johnston said.

"We can use your help," Roxborough replied. "We think Joe is ready for big things."

"Well," said Johnston matter-of-factly, evidently unaware Roxborough was black, "you understand he's a nigger, and he can't win every time he goes into the ring."

"So am I," the manager answered, and hung up.

A few years earlier, hanging up on Jimmy Johnston would have been hanging up on a career. Fortunately for Louis's sake, the Garden in 1934 was no longer the only show in town. Its monopoly was under siege, and leading the assault was a bluff, hustling promoter, "Uncle Mike" Jacobs (also known as

The making of a heavyweight: Lillie Reese Brooks watches over her son Joe at the family dinner table in Detroit.

"Uncle Wolf" because of his business habits as well as his technique with a knife and fork).

Born into poverty on New York's Lower West Side, Mike Jacobs spent his life in a tireless pursuit of money. Never really bothering with school, he found his calling in ticket promotion, working first as a "digger," a person who buys tickets at face value for a scalper, who resells them for a profit. Jacobs saw there was money in scalping, and by the time he was 15 he was in business for himself. In the 1920s, he ran the ticket-scalping operation for Tex Rickard, the head of Madison Square Garden and the top promoter of boxing. When Rickard died in 1929, the Garden's board of directors named Jimmy Johnston his successor, passing over Jacobs. Disappointed, Jacobs waited for his chance to even the score.

Johnston knew well enough to keep his eyes open. At the party in the Madison Square Garden Club given to celebrate Johnston's promotion, Jacobs pushed aside a waiter and served the beer himself. "Leave it to Mike to ace his way into the job that makes everybody come to *him*," Johnston snorted.

Jacobs's chance arrived in 1933, when three writers for the mammoth newspaper chain of William Randolph Hearst proposed a sweet little deal. As always, Jacobs asked, "What's in it for Uncle Mike?" Quite a lot, the writers said.

A dispute between Madison Square Garden and a charity headed by Hearst's wife had created an inviting opportunity. For years, the Garden had been staging boxing matches for Mrs. William Randolph Hearst's Free Milk Fund for Babies, and the Hearst newspapers had been returning the favor by blanketing their pages with free publicity for Garden events. This arrangement soured when the Garden, pressed for cash during the Great Depression, cut the Milk Fund's share of the take. The Hearsts were up in arms.

A new boxing promoter, pledging to restore the charity's old share, stood to grab the Milk Fund's boxing card from the Garden and pick up the invaluable backing of the Hearst chain. The three writers who approached Jacobs—the sports editors for two of Hearst's New York papers and the legendary Broadway columnist Damon Runyon—sought a large piece of the action. They wanted to be the promoter's silent partners, sharing in his profits while keeping their positions with Hearst and using their columns to

The author Damon Runyon (foreground) was one of three newspapermen to join forces with boxing promoter Mike Jacobs in a self-serving scheme to stage fights featuring Louis. Runyon and the others heavily publicized Louis in their newspaper articles during the mid-1930s, thereby creating an exceptional amount of interest in his fights.

boost the fights. And they wanted Mike Jacobs. He would handle the details of ticket sales and fight promotion, and, not least of all, he would shield the writers' identity.

The writers' scheme was surely unethical—and just as surely attractive to Jacobs. The four men formed a partnership, the Twentieth Century Sporting Club, and Jacobs leased the creaking old New York Hippodrome on 44th Street and 6th Avenue, where he started staging fights. Soon, he would be poised to dethrone Jimmy Johnston.

At about the same time, a pair of fight managers gave Jacobs a tip. "Mike, there's a kid fighting around Chicago name of Joe Louis you should get," said one.

"He's a heavyweight," added the other manager. "He'll be a champ."

"We'll see about it," Jacobs said.

Jacobs needed no one to tell him what a great heavyweight was worth. If he could get under contract a champion, or potential champion—a fighter people would pay top dollar to see—he would be well on his way to beating Johnston and the Garden at their own game.

In February 1935, Jacobs traveled to Los Angeles, where Louis was scheduled for a rematch with Lee Ramage, the fighter who had given him problems the previous December. Ramage was primed for revenge. Moreover, he was fighting in his hometown. Louis was warned he might not get a fair shake if the bout went to a decision. He made sure there was no chance of that. In the second round, he knocked Ramage out with a left hook to the jaw.

For Jacobs, those two rounds were worth the three-day train trip across the country. He was convinced he had seen the future heavyweight champion and immediately began courting Louis and his managers, taking care not to repeat Johnston's mistake. To Roxborough, he said, "John, you and Joe are colored. I'm a Jew. It's going to be hard for us to do anything. But if you stick with me I think I can do it." Jacobs pledged that every fight would be on the level: "He can win every fight he has, knock 'em out in the first round if possible. I promise if Joe ever gets to the top, he'll get a shot at the title." He was telling Louis and his managers precisely what they wanted to hear.

While Roxborough and Black considered Jacobs's offer, the promoter cranked up his publicity mill. His silent partners, the Hearst writers, filled the sports pages of their papers with glowing tributes to the wondrous new heavyweight. Earlier, a Detroit sportswriter had labeled Louis the Brown Bomber, and that became his moniker, with the Hearst chain leading the way in spreading it to the nation. Jacobs wanted to let the rest of the press in on his discovery, so he invited several dozen reporters to Detroit for Louis's March 28, 1935, fight with Natie Brown. Jacobs treated them to a first-class trip from New York, hiring a private railway car and stocking it with an inexhaustible supply of liquor and food.

Performing before some of the best-known sportswriters in the business, Louis was keyed up and overanxious. Natie Brown did not help matters. "He was clumsy and had an awkward style that would make anyone look bad," Louis recalled. He knocked Brown down in the first round but could not knock him out, winning the 10-round fight by a decision. Even on an off night he impressed the visiting press. "He is cold as ice and when he moves, he does so as would a tiger or a lion," raved Caswell Adams in the New York *Herald Tribune*.

After the fight, at a party to celebrate the victory, Jacobs brushed off Louis's apologies for his subpar performance. With Roxborough and Black at his side, Jacobs told Louis he thought he could promote him to the championship. Together, he said, they could make lots and lots of money.

"When my managers asked me how I felt about it," Louis said, "I told them they were the managers and what they said was fine with me." But the noise from the party made it hard for the older man to hear the soft-spoken boxer's response, so they retreated to the lavatory. There Jacobs produced the contract that made the Twentieth Century Sporting Club the sole promoter of Joe Louis's fights. Using the basin as a desk, Louis signed the contract. "It was a very long time before I figured how important a move this was," he reflected. "Jacobs was depending on me to be the next world's heavyweight champion."

Jacobs promptly got Louis a big fight. In the spring, the promoter announced that on June 25, 1935, Louis would battle the former heavyweight champion of the world, Primo Carnera, who had held the title in 1933 and 1934 and was recognized the world over. They would be squaring off in the best-known arena in sports, Yankee Stadium. It was a real step up.

Louis tuned up for Carnera by fighting five times in a space of four weeks during April and May. Facing woefully inferior opponents, he won each bout by a knockout. These fights sharpened Louis's skills, put him in peak condition, and, from Jacobs's perspective, kept the Brown Bomber in the headlines.

By the time he arrived in New York, Louis was a genuine celebrity. He was welcomed by Mayor Fiorello La Guardia, cheered by blacks in Harlem, and, day after day, pursued by reporters. At his first New York press conference, the spotlight of attention nearly blinded the 21-year-old fighter. "There were so many reporters, and cameras flashing, newsreels running," he remembered. "If I hadn't had my managers and Mike Jacobs there, I would have looked funny. I couldn't talk as fast as those reporters were talking."

International politics added an unwelcome tension to the bout. Carnera was an Italian, and in 1935

Mayor Fiorello La Guardia greets the most celebrated black athlete in America shortly after Louis arrived in New York for the first time. Several days later, in front of the country's largest fight crowd in five years, the heavyweight boxer scored an impressive victory over Primo Carnera at Yankee Stadium and established himself as the sport's top gate attraction.

the militaristic fascist regime of his homeland, led by Benito Mussolini, was threatening to invade Ethiopia, the oldest independent black nation on earth. With American blacks defending the Ethiopians and Italian Americans largely sympathetic to Mussolini, some feared trouble at Yankee Stadium, where, in the words of one reporter, "the crowd at this Italian-Negro prize fight will be composed largely of Italians . . . and Negroes from New York's Harlem section."

On the evening of June 25, partisans numbering 62,000 nearly filled the ballpark. Coming out of the dressing room and hearing the crowd roar, Louis was awestruck. It suddenly dawned on him how big the big time really was. "This was the best night in all of my fighting," he said years later. "If you was ever a raggedy kid and come to something like that night, you'd know. I don't thrill to things like other people. I only feel good. I felt the best that night."

There was small danger Carnera would spoil things. At 6 feet 6 inches and 260 pounds, he dwarfed his opponents and moved with a grace surprising for so large a man. But, in truth, he was not a very good fighter. "As underdone as a raw onion," one observer

said of him. Carnera's championship had been clouded
by a series of fixed fights and ties to the underworld.
(Not long before the showdown with Louis, he had
happily entertained the notorious gangster Al Capone,
then in prison.) Still, going into the fight, Carnera
was thought of as a powerful puncher, and the odds-
makers established Louis as just an 8–5 favorite.

It was no contest. Before the opening bell, Jack
Blackburn instructed Louis, "Go out and hit him in
the belly. His hands gonna come down. Then you
go for his head." Through five rounds, Louis alter-
nated between battering Carnera's body and head.
The Italian Goliath seldom retaliated. He only demonstrated a capacity to absorb punishment. In his
corner between the fifth and sixth rounds, pale and
bleeding, Carnera told his seconds, "I don't want any
more of that."

In the sixth, Louis unleashed a series of rights
that dropped Carnera off his feet. Gamely, he staggered up, only to be sent back down by another right
to the jaw. Struggling to his feet again seemed to
take the fight out of him; he placed his hands on the
ropes, and referee Arthur Donovan rushed in to halt
the contest. "What had started out as an Alp," said
one writer of Carnera, "looked about the altitude of
a chicken croquet by the time Joe got through with
him."

The police that night were braced for disturbances
between black and white spectators. There were none
to speak of. In Damon Runyon's view, Louis himself
had seen to that. "The whites applauded the amazing
performance of this youthful Negro more than the
blacks," he wrote the next day.

His destruction of Carnera confirmed Louis's
fame. Sportswriters and columnists wrote millions of
words about him, and they said almost unanimously
that he was the best heavyweight since Jack Dempsey,
the storied Manassa Mauler of the 1920s. The press
did not stop with accounts of Louis's boxing prowess.

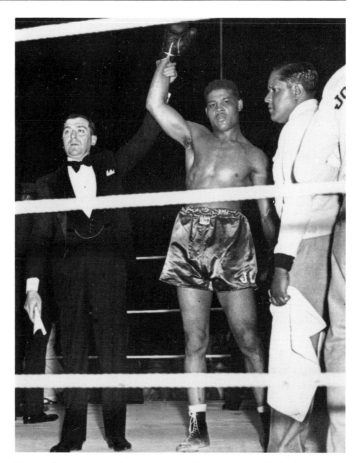

Louis is proclaimed the winner over former heavyweight title-holder Primo Carnera in June 1935. Marking his 23rd consecutive win, Louis's punishing sixth-round victory over the internationally known fighter convinced boxing experts that Louis would soon win the world heavyweight championship.

Everything was fair game—his personal habits, his character, and, above all else, his race.

The reporters covering Louis for the major metropolitan dailies were, generally speaking, agreeable fellows—chain-smoking, hard-drinking, card-playing regular guys. They were, without exception, white, and they were, to be blunt, racists.

Consider the lead sentence in a wire service account of the Carnera fight: "Something sly and sinister and perhaps not quite human came out of the African jungle last night to strike down and utterly demolish the huge hulk that had been Primo Carnera, the giant." Or consider the nicknames reporters not satisfied with "Brown Bomber" tossed into their stories. At one time or another, Louis was "the dark dynamiter," "the mahogany maimer," "the sable cyclone," "the dusky downer," "Mike Jacobs's pet pickaninny," "the shufflin' shadow," "the sepia slugger," "the tawny tiger-cat," "the coffee colored kayo king," "the murder man of those maroon mitts," "the tan-skinned terror," "the chocolate chopper," "the tan Tarzan of thump."

Few whites saw anything particularly offensive in these characterizations. They were simply the sort of thing whites said about blacks in the 1930s. Indeed, the reporters liked Louis and went out of their way to praise his quiet, unassuming manner. He knew his place and served as a fine role model for black America. "Joe Louis is a non-pretentious, self-effacing lad and a credit to his race," wrote columnist Jack O'Brien. "Unlike Jack Johnson, Joe is as clean as a hound tooth. One can get an insight to his character when they remember he stated the other day that his favorite book is the Bible."

The Bible reading was a fiction dreamed up by one of Mike Jacobs's press agents, but what was genuine and what stood out so sharply against the bigotry of the press was the natural decency and dignity of the young man from Detroit. Before the bout with Carnera, some photographers came to a photo session at Louis's training camp with a sliced watermelon. "One of them tried to have Joe Louis pose with this watermelon," remembered someone who was there. " 'Great shot, Joe. Make a great shot.' And Louis wouldn't do it. Now nobody told him not to, but instinctively he knew that this was a racist kind of thing and he wouldn't do it. And they kept saying, 'Well, why not, Joe? Make a great shot, Joe, great shot.' "

The observer heard Louis respond, "I don't like watermelon."

"Well, he loved watermelon." ❧

5

"CHAPPIE,
THIS IS IT"

MIKE HAD NO prejudice about a man's color so long as he could make a green buck for him," Joe Louis said of his promoter. With Primo Carnera disposed of, Jacobs promptly lined up another blockbuster fight with another former champion. In September 1935, again at Yankee Stadium, Louis was to face Max Baer. Less that two weeks before Louis's victory over Carnera, Baer had lost the heavyweight title to James J. Braddock. Out of shape, the 26-year-old Baer had played the clown in the ring with Braddock and had only himself to blame for losing. When in condition, he was a good fighter, better than any Louis had met so far.

In August, as a tune-up for Baer, Louis fought King Levinsky in Chicago, knocking him out in the first round. Levinsky was beaten before the opening bell. Terrified by all he had read and heard about Louis's punching power, he was so genuinely fearful in his dressing room that Mike Jacobs worried they might not get him to the ring. To keep Levinsky from bolting, Jacobs moved the starting time of the fight up a half hour. The bout ended with Levinsky sitting on the middle strand of the ropes, begging the referee, "Don't let him hit me again."

Louis, flanked on his right by Jack Blackburn and on his left by Julian Black, raises the fist that knocked the heavyweight crown off the head of James J. Braddock a few moments earlier. The title bout took place on June 22, 1937, in Chicago's Comiskey Park.

As September neared, Louis's thoughts were not altogether on Max Baer. Louis had always enjoyed the attention of women, and their advances grew bolder as the list of his victories lengthened. One day, after the Carnera fight, Louis dropped in at the Buick dealership in Detroit. He was intrigued by a black sedan with custom coachwork and a mahogany bar in the backseat. As he examined the car, his salesman excused himself and walked across the showroom to speak with an attractive woman with blonde hair. When the man finally returned, Louis had made up his mind; he wanted to buy the car.

"The lady has already purchased the car for you," the salesman replied.

All the warnings about Jack Johnson and of avoiding the company of white women rushed through Louis's head. He tried to refuse the woman's offer but found himself unable to resist her charms. "I took the car," he remembered, "and promised her two ringside tickets for the Max Baer fight."

The most frequent passenger in Louis's Buick during 1935 was Marva Trotter, a beautiful young secretary he had met in Chicago. She had come to the gym to watch him train; in her words, "I gave the big man a once over. It was love at first sight." Intelligent and ambitious, she captured Louis's affections. Although he continued seeing other women, Marva was someone special. "Oh, I was crazy about those sweet beauties, but I loved Marva," he said. His mother treated her like one of the family, and his managers encouraged him to lay to rest the memory of Jack Johnson by marrying such a pleasant black woman. Julian Black told him, "Man, you're in love with Marva. Marry her."

At 7:45 on the evening of September 24, 1935, at a friend's apartment in Harlem, Joe Louis did. The ceremony was performed by the bride's brother, a minister, and was necessarily brief. At 8:00 P.M.,

Louis's first wife, the former Marva Trotter, steps into the couple's Duesenberg roadster. They were married on September 24, 1935—the same evening that Louis fought Max Baer.

Louis pushed his way out of the apartment, through a throng of well-wishers in the street, and into a waiting limousine. Escorted by police squad cars, their sirens wailing, he was whisked away to Yankee Stadium. He would be fighting Max Baer on his wedding night.

The fight drew nearly 90,000 to the stadium—the largest crowd ever to see a boxing event in New York, with the spectators paying more than a million dollars for their tickets. The enormous gate was the work of Mike Jacobs, who, according to the writer Budd Schulberg, "kept an eye on his ticket sale the way an old man does on an attractive young wife." The Buick Motor Company, makers of Louis's preferred automobile, paid a whopping $27,500 for radio rights on the NBC network.

Wearing trunks embroidered with a Star of David proclaiming his Jewish heritage, Baer looked splendid as he entered the ring. Tipping the scales at 210¼ pounds, he outweighed Louis by 11 pounds. From his corner, Louis spotted his bride at ringside and decided

Former champion Max Baer takes a hard left to the chin as Louis clears his own path to the heavyweight crown. Baer became the second titleholder to fall to Louis within a three-month span in 1935.

it had to be a short fight: "I wanted to start being a married man as soon as possible."

Baer was a good fighter, but it made no difference. Louis tore him to pieces. His short jab fired over and over like a steel piston. Each time it landed on Baer's face, his head snapped backward. Baer did not even try to mix it up. "He just wasn't right," Louis recalled. "I don't know what happened to him that night."

What happened was that Baer was scared to death of his expressionless foe. In the fourth round, Louis belted him with a left hook and followed it with a quick right to the head. Baer went down but not out. By the time the referee counted six, he had risen to one knee. "Baer's on one knee, seven, eight, nine," shouted Clem McCarthy, describing the count for the NBC audience. "Baer is not up, and Baer is on his knee at the count of ten. Your fight is all over; your fight is all over. The boys are coming into the ring with the speed of a Buick. Of a new Buick." Although able to continue, Baer had decided to surrender. "I could have struggled up once more," he said later, "but when I get executed, people are going to have to pay more than twenty-five dollars a seat to watch it."

In Harlem, they celebrated until dawn. "Milling thousands of Negro men, women and children turned the district into bedlam as they surged through the streets, howling gleefully, blowing horns, dancing madly, pounding on pots and pans," reported the New York *Sun*. In black neighborhoods from New York to California, this sort of demonstration became a ritual after Louis's victories. At a time when blacks were barred from major league baseball, when football rosters were nearly all white, and when blacks in films were always playing servants or slaves, Louis was the one black with the same chance as a white for fame and fortune. Listening by their radios or whooping it up in the streets, black Americans dreamed of the not-far-off day when one of their own would be the heavyweight champion of the world.

In December, Louis moved a step closer to the title with a conquest of Paolino Uzcudun, "the Basque Woodchopper." Although never a champion, nor a real threat to become one, Uzcudun fought in a perplexing "peekaboo" style—both gloves in front of his face, his elbows held tight to the body. The style did not allow for much offensive power, but in a long career he had never been knocked out. For three rounds, Louis doggedly pursued him, unable to land a clean blow. Then, in the fourth, Uzcudun parted his gloves for an instant, and Louis pounced. He struck a right to the jaw that smashed two of Uzcudun's teeth through his lower lip, lifted him off his feet, and pitched him to the other side of the ring. He was out cold. "I can't begin to describe that punch . . . this was the hardest punch I've ever seen thrown," remembered a veteran fight reporter who was at ringside that evening.

For Louis, his managers, and his promoter, things were going flawlessly. Mike Jacobs appeared to have Jimmy Johnston and Madison Square Garden over a barrel. Jacobs had Louis, the heavyweight fighter people were clamoring to see, while Johnston had James J. Braddock, the weakest champion in memory, the loser of 26 fights in his career—a box-office dud. Sooner or later, if Louis kept winning, Johnston, for the sake of a huge gate, would be forced to match his champion with the Brown Bomber. And most likely sooner. By early 1936, Louis had cleared the deck of every serious challenger save one: a former champion who had been languishing in semiretirement, Germany's Max Schmeling.

Jacobs arranged a fight between Louis and Schmeling at Yankee Stadium in June 1936, with the winner getting a shot at Braddock and the title. A clause in their contract barred Schmeling and Louis from fighting during the six months prior to the bout.

A fight-weary Louis on tour with his Brown Bombers softball team. The boxer formed the barnstorming squad with his boyhood friends to help them earn some money during the Great Depression.

For Louis, who had been doing little else but fighting for three years, it was a welcome respite. Now, for a while, he had the time and, in fantastic amounts, the money to enjoy life. In 1934, for his first professional fight, he had earned $59; for his 25th, the victory over Baer, he collected $240,000. In the mid-1930s, when a new Chevrolet cost $700 and 95 percent of the work force earned less than $2,500 a year, Joe Louis was very, very rich.

For Louis, it was easy come, easy go. "When he would come to Detroit," recalled one of his brothers, "he'd always have a stack of $10 bills, and he would just pass them out to everybody." He purchased a new house for his mother, and for his old neighborhood buddies he bought uniforms, equipment, and a bus, thereby creating the Brown Bombers traveling softball team. He and Marva moved into a spacious apartment in Chicago's finest all-black building, where the rooms were a decorator's showpiece and the closets bulged with her mink coats and his suits. As fast as Louis's hands were in the ring, they were even faster reaching for the check at a restaurant. No one ever managed to grab it from him, and his extravagant tips left more than a few waiters speechless.

Louis loved Marva deeply, but he did not let marriage interfere with his habits. Although his wife was socially ambitious and preferred the company of the refined black middle class, he stayed close to his old friends—people whom Marva regarded as crude parasites. Nor did he particularly alter his love life. Mindful of Jack Johnson, he was discreet, but he nevertheless made the rounds.

The sudden fame had gone to Louis's head. "I can't go wrong. I got the money, I got the power," he remembered thinking. A perfectly understandable attitude for a 22 year old flushed with success, it was really not the best frame of mind for getting ready to fight Max Schmeling.

At his training camp in Lakewood, New Jersey, Louis acted as if he knew more than Jack Blackburn did and started cutting short his workouts for trips to the golf course. New to the game—and hooked on it—he played round after round when he should have been sparring or punching the heavy bag. "Chappie, that ain't good for you," Blackburn warned him of golf. "The timing's different. And them muscles you use in golf, they ain't the same ones you use hitting a man. Besides, being out in the sun don't do you no good. You'll be dried out." Louis ignored him, figuring he could name the round in which he was going to knock Schmeling out.

Meanwhile, Schmeling pushed himself into imposing shape. He had been at ringside for the Louis-Uzcudun fight, and he said confidently when leaving the stadium, "I see something." All anyone else could see was a human thunderbolt, but Schmeling believed he had spotted a flaw in Louis's style. Weeks of carefully studying the films of the fight, frame by frame, convinced him that he was onto something. Louis, after throwing a left, dropped his left hand too low, leaving him open for an opponent's right. With a choreographer's precision, Schmeling worked out a strategy of moving with Louis's right, to lessen its

Louis on a Hollywood set in the spring of 1936, filming The Spirit of Youth. *The story of a dishwasher who rises to become a world champion boxer, the movie was loosely based on Louis's life.*

impact, and of launching his own right the second after Louis jabbed or hooked with his left.

Forty thousand people turned up at Yankee Stadium on June 19, 1936, a night threatened by rain. Among them, in a good seat, was Lillie Barrow Brooks. She was looking forward to seeing her son fight for the first time. There was no question of Louis's victory. How long could Schmeling last? was all that was being asked.

Before the bell, Blackburn gave Louis some last-second advice: "For God's sake, keep your left arm high." As in training camp, Louis did not listen. After the first round, he told Chappie that Schmeling was a pushover.

In the second, when Louis fired a left hook, Schmeling came back with a right. It landed squarely on Louis's chin. For a second, he thought he had swallowed his mouthpiece.

In the fourth, after a Louis left, another Schmeling right came crashing in, sending Louis down. He could not believe it had happened; he was sprawled on his backside, and his jaw felt broken. The astonished crowd erupted with cheers. Louis scrambled to his feet, but he was dazed.

After the sixth round—and another assault from Schmeling's right—Louis's longtime friend Freddie Guinyard led a sobbing Lillie Barrow from the stadium. "My God, my God, don't let them kill my child," she cried.

Louis was in a fog. Somehow, he lasted until the 12th round, when Schmeling threw everything he had, as many as 50 rights. The last one knocked Louis out.

Bruised, barely able to open his eyes, he held a straw hat over his swollen face when he left the ballpark. Louis was in seclusion for days, ashamed to let anyone see the beating he had taken. "He got into bed fully dressed and lay there like a mummy refusing to speak," Marva recalled.

On the ropes: Louis kneels on the canvas, trying unsuccessfully to shake off the effects of a right uppercut by Max Schmeling in their first meeting. Losing the fight temporarily cost Louis a shot at the heavyweight title.

"Man, Harlem was a sad and sorry place," said a longtime resident, describing the mood after Louis's loss. "Not only was it a sad place, it was a dangerous place to be in. People were distraught and very, very edgy. You were subject to being really hurt if you crossed anybody in the wrong way. Man, Joe Louis was such an idol and it was assumed he could not lose." Another Harlemite said, "Dear God, we all went into mourning."

Mike Jacobs was a little down himself. Now Schmeling, not Louis, was the number one contender and had the claim to a championship fight with Braddock. On the strength of Schmeling's roundhouse right, the advantage had swung back to Johnston and Madison Square Garden. Jacobs, however, was never one to throw in the towel, and with his usual energy he scrambled to reestablish his man.

The first order of business was to get his fighter out of seclusion and back into the ring. This was accomplished by booking Yankee Stadium for August 18, 1936, and scheduling a fight with Jack Sharkey, yet another former champion—the man who had taken the title from Schmeling in 1932.

Fight fans watch Louis during a workout at his training camp in Pompton Lakes, New Jersey. After losing to Max Schmeling in June 1936, Louis proceeded to train harder than ever before.

In training camp, Louis was back to his old self, working hard, listening to Blackburn. In the ring at the stadium before the fight, the young boxer was uncharacteristically nervous. "My career was at stake," he said. "I couldn't afford to lose two fights in a row."

Sharkey, as expected, emulated Schmeling, throwing nothing but rights. To no avail. In the third round, Louis knocked him out with a right of his own. Blackburn told the press, "Joe's mad at Schmeling, but Sharkey paid for it."

As did a host of other fighters. Attempting to rebuild his reputation, Louis fought almost constantly. Between September 1936 and February 1937, he took part in 10 fights, including 4 exhibitions. He won 9 by knockout. Only one, a 10-round battle with Bob Pastor, went the distance. (Jimmy Johnston had instructed Pastor, who was under contract to Madison Square Garden, to keep moving: "Louis can't hit you if you don't stand still." Pastor took the advice and never allowed Louis a clean shot. Although Louis won, Pastor succeeded in making him appear awkward.) A more typical Louis fight took place at Cleveland in December 1936, when he knocked out Eddie Simms, nailing him with a left hook only 26 seconds into the first round.

For a while, it looked as if Louis could knock the world out and not get a chance at the championship. Braddock and Schmeling contracted with Madison Square Garden to fight for the title, setting the date for June 3, 1937. Mike Jacobs knew that if the fight took place and if Schmeling won, as seemed likely, Louis would be done for. The German would never risk a rematch with Louis. So Jacobs did his best to sabotage the Braddock-Schmeling affair. He encouraged anti-Nazi groups to organize boycotts of Schmeling fights and warned that the heavyweight title was on the verge of becoming a possession of Adolf Hitler.

Jacobs's heavy work was done behind the scenes. His actions had nothing to do with international politics and everything to do with old-fashioned deals. No sooner was the ink dry on the contract between Schmeling and Braddock than Jacobs began a courtship of the champion's manager, Joe Gould. Described by Budd Schulberg as a "managerial Fred Astaire, who could spin so rapidly that no one was ever able to tell in which direction he was really looking," Gould had in common with Jacobs an eye for the main chance. While everyone awaited the Braddock-Schmeling fight, Gould shopped his boxer to the highest bidder. Johnston pledged to increase Gould's cut of the gate if he honored the contract with the Garden. The Nazis chimed in with a lucrative offer for Braddock and Schmeling to fight in Germany.

Mike Jacobs trumped every ace. He made a deal with Gould and Braddock that guaranteed them a cool $500,000 for a fight with Louis, and if the champion should lose, 10 percent of Jacobs's net profits from heavyweight fights for the next 10 years. It was an enormous price, yet Jacobs, with faith in Louis, knew it was worth it.

Schmeling fumed and Johnston hauled Jacobs into court, but Jacobs's deal with Gould held. On June 22, 1937, Louis and Braddock met for the heavyweight championship of the world in Comiskey Park, a baseball stadium on the South Side of Chicago.

James J. Braddock was the classic underdog. A journeyman boxer who had lost a lot of bouts, he had never earned enough in the ring to support his big family and for a while had been on relief. When finally given a fight with champion Max Baer in 1935, he told his wife he would "bring home the title." Hearing this, his many children leaped for joy. They thought he had said "turtle."

True to his word, Braddock wound up taking the

Rival boxing promoters Jimmy Johnston (left) of Madison Square Garden and Mike Jacobs (right) of the Twentieth Century Sporting Club put the squeeze on Max Schmeling's manager, Joe Jacobs. Schmeling eventually contracted with Madison Square Garden to fight the current heavyweight champion, James J. Braddock, in June 1937. Mike Jacobs sabotaged that deal, however, and arranged for Louis to face Braddock for the title instead.

Referee Tommy Thomas sends Louis to a neutral corner (above) as James J. Braddock attempts to lift himself off the canvas in the eighth round of their championship fight. A few minutes later, Louis raised his right hand in triumph (opposite) at the announcement that he had won claim to the title of heavyweight champion of the world.

championship from Baer. He was transformed by the press into the Cinderella Man, but success never spoiled him. "He was a wonderful guy," said his sparring partner George Nicholson. "Always treated everybody the same. When we put rocks in the beds of the guys at training camp, we would put them in his too. We ate together, showered together, all equals."

Braddock's good nature meant little to Louis and his handlers. "Chappie, this is it. You come home a champ tonight," Blackburn whispered to Louis in the ring as 45,000 fans packed Comiskey Park. The lustiest cheering arose from the bleachers, where a throng of nearly 20,000 blacks stood on their $3 seats shouting encouragement to their hero, awaiting the moment he would be crowned the heavyweight king.

Proud and gallant, Braddock gave it his best. In the first round, he smashed a right to Louis's jaw that floored the challenger. "What the hell am I doing here?" Louis asked himself. He bounced up before the referee could count three. It was Braddock's last hurrah. The rest of the fight was all Louis.

"I could have finished him anytime after the first round," Louis said, but Blackburn wanted caution. "He'll come apart in five or six rounds," the trainer instructed. "Take it easy. I'll tell you when to shoot." Taking it easy only prolonged Braddock's agony. By the fifth round, Louis was landing brutal shots at will, one splitting open the champion's lip, others bloodying his cheeks and brow.

Braddock was a wreck. In his corner after the seventh round, Joe Gould said he was going to throw in the towel. Through lips that were spurting blood, Braddock said, "If you do, I'll never speak to you as long as I live."

It ended in the eighth. Louis jabbed Braddock with a left to the head, a left to the body, and then drilled an overhand right to the chin that lifted the champion off his feet and whirled him forward. He landed face down. Braddock later said it felt "like someone nailed you with a crowbar. I thought half my head was blowed off."

When the referee reached the count of 10, the world had a new heavyweight champion.

In his dressing room, amid pandemonium, the new champion nearly fainted. All Joe Louis remembered saying was, "Bring on Max Schmeling. Bring him on."

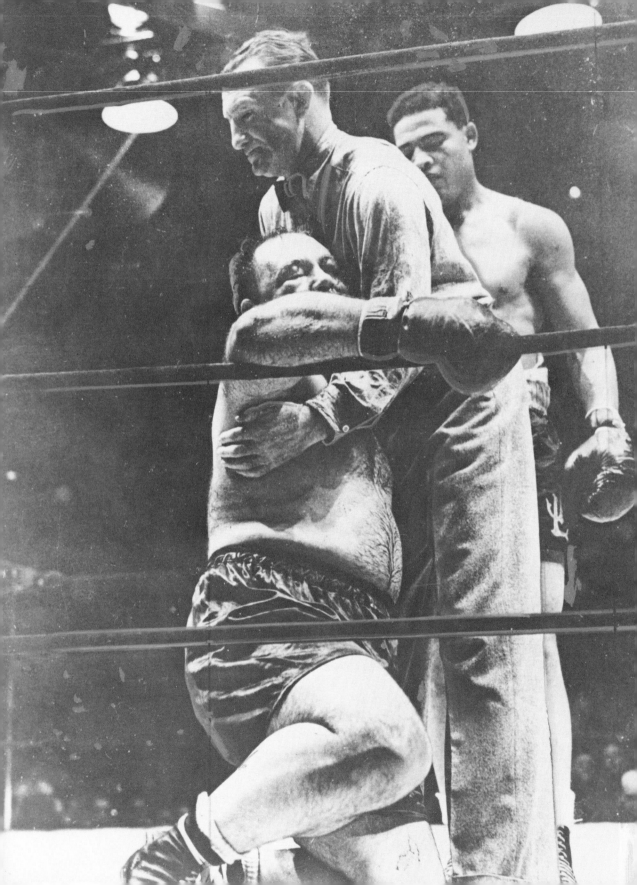

6

"THE BUM OF
THE MONTH
CLUB"

Louis watches Tony Galento cling to referee Barney Nagler for dear life in the fourth round of their June 1939 championship fight. Galento was one of the first members of the Bum of the Month Club, a collection of journeyman fighters who were soundly defeated by Louis.

IT IS A wonder anyone fought Joe Louis a second time. During his professional career, he faced 10 fighters twice and won every rematch, nearly always by a knockout. He was a patient, almost methodical fighter, stalking his foe, wearing him down, awaiting a mistake, then swiftly moving in for the kill. Sometimes, an entire fight passed without Louis finding an opening. But it never happened twice. For Joe Louis, winning a rematch was a matter of pride.

No one had wounded Louis's pride more deeply than Max Schmeling had, and no one paid a worse price for having done so. In two minutes, four seconds of the first round on June 22, 1938, Louis, in the words of sportswriter Bill Corum, had reduced "a proud and perfectly trained athlete into a quivering, quaking, beaten old man." The next morning, a rumor swept New York that Schmeling was dead. It was, of course, untrue, but he did spend two painful weeks in a New York hospital nursing a broken back before being carried by ambulance to a ship sailing for Germany. He never fought in the United States again.

Louis's victory over Schmeling triggered celebrations in black homes and neighborhoods around the country. "Everyone in Harlem who could walk was out on the street five minutes after the fight ended," the New York *Herald Tribune* reported. People waved

Joe Louis for President signs, and when the shouting was done the "streets were littered with everything from confetti to stringbeans."

There was rejoicing in unexpected places, too. In the lobby of a hotel in Mississippi, the most rigidly segregated state in the Union, a small crowd listened intently to Clem McCarthy's call of the fight on NBC. When it was over and Louis had smashed a symbol of Nazi Germany, remembered a woman who was at the hotel, the "white patrons and colored bellhops hugged each other in joy."

For Louis, the victory over Schmeling was the absolute peak of his career. "I had the championship, and I had beaten the man who had humiliated me," he recalled. "America was proud of me, my people were proud of me, and since the fight, race relations were lightening up—who the hell could ask for more?"

The Schmeling fight also paid well. From total gate receipts of $1,015,012, Louis received a check for just under $350,000. Julian Black, John Roxbor-

Louis's victory over Max Schmeling spurs a riotous celebration in New York City's black district of Harlem. Upon winning the 1938 match against the German fighter, Louis became known as "the first American to kayo a Nazi."

ough, and Jack Blackburn all drew their shares from Louis, as eventually did the Internal Revenue Service (IRS). Yet the champion was left with a lot of money. First Lady Eleanor Roosevelt, in her newspaper column the day after the fight, said she and the president hoped Louis "has some wise member of his family who takes his money and puts it away so that when he no longer has any opponents he will be able to do something else to make life interesting and pleasant."

Indeed, Louis had heard all sorts of sensible advice about insurance and safe, long-term investments. But he preferred to spend his money. As a reward for licking Schmeling, he went on a buying spree. His most spectacular purchase was Spring Hill, a sprawling 477-acre horse farm not far from Detroit. Fond of horseback riding, he kept two thoroughbreds, Jocko and Flash, and when he mounted them he was decked out in custom-made English boots and habit.

Playing the country squire did not come cheaply. When added to other spending, it strained Louis's bank account. Mike Jacobs was always happy to ease the pinch by loaning Louis whatever he needed to make ends meet.

Jacobs had every reason to stroke the champion. His fists had won for the promoter a mastery of professional boxing. Not long after Louis became champion, the directors of Madison Square Garden swallowed their pride, fired Jimmy Johnston, and brought in Jacobs as director of boxing. Jacobs consolidated his position at the top by dumping his three silent partners, the writers from the Hearst papers. He did so by leaking the details of their involvement with the Twentieth Century Sporting Club to the rival Scripps-Howard chain, which happily rushed into print with the story of reporters writing about fights they themselves were secretly promoting. Their conflict of interest exposed, the writers had little choice but to let Jacobs buy them out cheaply at $25,000 each.

Joe Gould, Braddock's manager, presented another problem. After all, he held a contract giving him 10 percent of Jacobs's net proceeds from heavyweight fights for 10 years. Jacobs acted as if he had never heard the word *contract* and refused to pay Gould a cent. Gould stirred up a fuss, threatened lawsuits, and eventually settled for the cash Jacobs offered him to forget about their deal.

"I will fight whenever and whoever Mike Jacobs wants me to," Louis said after taking the championship. Knowing the public could not see Louis often enough, Jacobs wanted him in the ring all the time. Roxborough and Black felt the same way, arguing that for a black champion to be fully accepted he needed to defend his title against all comers, and never, ever, could he be perceived as ducking an opponent.

A fighting champion was a dramatic break with tradition. Previous heavyweight champions had been notoriously inactive, preferring not to risk losing the most prestigious title in sports. Jack Dempsey, for instance, fought only five times during his seven-year reign, once going three years without a bout. Braddock, champion for two years, stepped into the ring only once—against Louis. Between August 1928 and June 1937, nearly nine years, there had been exactly seven heavyweight championship fights.

Louis changed all that. In one year alone, 1941, he fought seven times. From the day he won the title, June 22, 1937, until March 1942, Louis defended his championship an incredible 21 times, sometimes as often as once a month. It was a bonanza for the mediocre heavyweights of the world, with nearly every fighter who wanted a title shot getting one. In his rise to glory, Louis had cleaned out the top names in the heavyweight division, knocking out four for-

Louis signs a contract to box against his good friend John Henry Lewis, a former light-heavyweight champion, in January 1939. The match marked the first time ever that two blacks fought each other for the heavyweight title.

mer champions on his way to the title and a fifth, Schmeling, a year into his reign. That left, as they rather unfairly came to be called, "the Bums of the Month."

Louis's first foe after Schmeling was hardly a bum. John Henry Lewis had held the light-heavyweight championship for the best part of four years and was a good friend of Louis's. "I knew I wasn't going to lose nothing and John Henry at least could make a decent buck," Louis explained.

Louis versus Lewis made history. For the first time, two blacks fought for a championship. Otherwise, their fight on January 25, 1939, at Madison Square Garden was unmemorable. One of the oldest maxims in boxing is that a good big man will beat a good smaller man every time, and Joe outweighed John Henry by 20 pounds. "When I went in the ring that night, I remember thinking to myself, I'm not gonna punish John, I'm gonna try to get this over in a hurry," Louis remembered. The challenger went down three times in the first round before the referee stopped the contest.

"I'll moider da bum," predicted Tony Galento prior to his June 1939 fight with Louis. Galento did this boasting in his New Jersey tavern, where he entertained customers by opening beer bottles with his teeth. Standing 5 feet 9 inches, weighing 225 pounds, Two-Ton Tony, the Walking Beer Barrel trained when he felt like it but ate and guzzled all the time. Once, before a fight, on a bet, he wolfed down 50 frankfurters and grew so bloated that his trainer had to slit open the waistband of his boxing trunks for him to squeeze them on.

Galento possessed neither the knowledge nor the skill of a boxer, but he could fight. His left hook, slow and ponderous, packed a tremendous wallop, and, best of all for someone facing Louis, he could take a punch. He had never been knocked down.

Nearly 40,000 turned up at Yankee Stadium on June 28, 1939, for Louis against Galento. Watching the fighters warm up, the crowd must be forgiven for expecting a complete mismatch. In one corner, Louis, as he always did, appeared in top condition, his chest and shoulders massive, his stomach absolutely flat, the powerful muscles of his arms and legs buried beneath smooth brown skin. Galento, on the other hand, looked like a torpedo in a bathing suit.

Annoyed by Galento's taunts and enraged by his shouting an obscenity about Marva just before the bell, Louis came out smoking, determined to make an early night of it. Two-Ton Tony had other ideas. Fighting out of a low crouch, he tagged the champion with his left hook. "Everything glazed over," Louis said. Covering up, denying the wildly swinging Galento a target, Louis recovered and just before the end of round one staggered the challenger with a left-right combination. Things went according to form in the second round, as Louis punished Galento, once hitting him hard enough to nearly lift him off the canvas, another time smashing a right to his jaw that put him down.

In the third round, Louis picked up where he had left off. Galento, wobbling around, was bleeding profusely. Suddenly, when coming out of a clinch, Galento fired his last shot, and it was a beauty. A left hook caught Louis at the very tip of his chin and knocked him onto his backside. The Yankee Stadium throng, having seen the impossible, erupted into bedlam. The "funny little fat man," as Louis called Galento, had drilled the champion. Stunned but unhurt, Louis was back on his feet as the referee counted two.

The champion's pride had been damaged. In the fourth round, as angry as he had ever been in the ring, he finished Galento off. "The hardest punches I ever saw Louis throw were against Galento," said veteran fight correspondent Barney Nagler. "Every time he hit him it made little breaks in the skin as though he cut himself shaving." When the end came, referee Arthur Donovan recalled, "Galento went down with his feet sticking straight up in the air."

In 1940, Louis fought four times, twice against Arturo Godoy, a Chilean heavyweight virtually unknown in the United States. By the time of their first match, on February 9, the grueling, seemingly endless schedule of fights had begun to catch up with Louis. "I really dogged it," he said. "I didn't feel peppy.

In 1940, Louis fought Arturo Godoy twice within a span of five months. In their first meeting, the Chilean heavyweight attempted to wear down the champion by boxing in an exaggerated crouch that provided Louis with an extremely small target; Godoy managed to last the distance, although he lost the fight. Louis had perfected his uppercut by the time of their second match, however, and he used it with devastating effect, ending the slugfest by sending Godoy to his knees in the eighth round.

Godoy had a funny crouch, and he was hard to hit; but that wasn't all that was wrong. I had no heart for fighting that night. That's why he stayed fifteen rounds." Evidently elated at going the distance with the champion, Godoy raced across the ring at the fight's conclusion and attempted to give Louis a kiss. Disgusted by both his performance and by the Chilean's gesture, Louis brushed him away. "I ain't never had no man kiss me," he growled.

Their second encounter on June 20 at Yankee Stadium was a different story. In training camp, Louis had perfected his uppercut, just the punch for lifting Godoy out of his crouch. By the eighth round, Godoy was a bloody mess, and when the champion dropped him to his knees, the referee ended the fight. Again, Godoy rushed to Louis, this time with no intention of giving him a kiss but with every thought of continuing the fight. "With imperial calm," wrote Nat Fleischer, the founder of *Ring* magazine, "Joe turned his back, started through the ropes, and motioned to his trainer, Jack Blackburn, to take care of Godoy."

Louis disliked hearing his series of opponents called the Bum of the Month Club. "Those guys I fought were not bums," he insisted. "They were hardworking professionals trying to make a dollar, too." In the ring against Louis, though, it was often hard to tell the difference. From December 1940 until June 1941, he defended his title once a month—seven months, seven fights. They were mostly forgettable affairs. In quick order, he knocked out Al McCoy, Red Burman, Gus Dorazio, Abe Simon, and Tony Musto. They generated nothing remotely like the excitement that preceded the second Schmeling fight, and it showed at the gate. Louis's largest purse was a meager $21,000 for the bout with Burman.

Louis's opponent for May 1941, Buddy Baer, the brother of the former champion, at least got off to a fast start. During the first round, the 6'6¼" Baer cleanly landed a 3-punch combination that, to the crowd's astonishment, sent Louis reeling backward clear through the ropes and onto the apron of the ring. He climbed back before the count of four, an embarrassed and angry fighter. He proceeded to pound the daylights out of Baer. In the sixth, the challenger fell to the canvas three times and was unable to answer the bell beginning the seventh round.

The Bum of the Month campaign skidded to an abrupt halt when Louis faced Billy Conn on the evening of June 18, 1941, at the Polo Grounds in New York. Conn was everything the other challengers were not. He was small, fast, and clever. Louis against Conn was the fight everyone had been waiting for, and the 2 principals did not disappoint a soul among the 55,000 who filled the old horseshoe-shaped stadium in upper Manhattan. "No better and greater fight did anyone ever see," said Bill Corum on the radio at the moment the battle ended. In all the years since, Corum's judgment has gone undisputed.

"A Celtic God," raved the actor Alfred Lunt describing Conn. Not quite, but he was cocky, Irish, and wonderfully handsome. He hailed from Pittsburgh and, like all his friends, started out fighting in the streets. After staying two years in the eighth grade, he turned to boxing, winding up under the wing of Johnny Ray, the best trainer in town, who guided Conn to impressive victories in and around Pittsburgh. The young fighter caught the ever-alert eye of Mike Jacobs, who rapidly promoted Conn's speed and skill into the light-heavyweight championship.

Conn then set his sights on the heavyweight crown, even though he only weighed 170 pounds. With dazzling footwork and lightning punches, he blazed by several heavyweight contenders. Jacobs figured he was ready for a shot at Louis.

Louis took the buildup for Conn calmly. By June, the heavyweight champion had heard enough about the challenger's quickness. "He can run, but he can't hide," Louis said.

But Conn nearly did. By round three, he was grinning at Louis, daring the champion to hit him. By the end of the fourth round, Conn was laughing as he headed to his corner. "This is a cinch," he said breezily to Johnny Ray. He had bicycled around the ring during the round, making Louis look slow; for a few moments, he had even stayed still, slugging it out. As if awakened by a cold shower, Louis stormed back in the next three rounds, rocking Conn again and again.

The tide turned once more in the eighth. Louis was visibly tired, but Conn looked as fresh as ever, darting away from Louis's jabs, then swiftly counterpunching. As the bell ended the ninth round, Conn called out, "Joe, you're in a fight tonight."

"I know it," Louis replied. He was in severe trouble, and it was not the sort he had got into from the lumbering right of Schmeling, or the lucky Sunday punches of Braddock, Galento, and Buddy Baer. Conn's hands were so fast he was beating Louis to the punch. On the judges' scorecards, the challenger had pulled ahead.

It got worse for Louis. In the 12th round, he recalled, "I was completely exhausted and he was really hurting me with left hooks." In the last minute of the round, Conn landed a left that nearly knocked Louis off the heavyweight throne. On the Mutual Radio Network, Don Dunphy described the sensational action: "Louis is staggered by a left hook. Conn staggers Louis. . . . Louis is reeling around and holding on. A left hook to the jaw followed by a right cross, and the champion is hurt. Louis is trying to hold on."

He managed to get through the round. As he wobbled to his corner, his eyes glassy, he looked like

One of the most exciting bouts in Louis's career took place on June 18, 1941, against the remarkably quick and clever Billy Conn. Able to dance away from Louis's blows, the challenger dominated the fight until the end of the 13th round, when Louis threw a right cross that stopped Conn in his tracks. The two boxers are shown here in their heavyweight title rematch five years later, with Louis again chasing after Conn. This time, the heavyweight champion knocked out Conn with a right uppercut and a left hook in the eighth round.

a beaten fighter. He slumped onto his stool. Jack Blackburn yanked out his mouthpiece and rubbed the champion's head. "Chappie, you're *losing*," he said. "You got to knock him out." There was no other way; if the fight went to a decision, Conn would win.

Across the ring, Conn, sitting on his stool, said, "This is easy." He promised Ray a knockout in the next round.

"No, no, Billy," Ray screamed. "Stick and run. You got the fight won. Stay away, kiddo. Just stick and run, stick and run." Conn did not listen. He did not want to be the man who beat Joe Louis. He wanted to be the man who knocked Joe Louis out.

It was a terrible mistake because Louis was waiting for him. Somehow, the champion had found a last reserve of energy, and that, combined with his formidable pride, was enough to see him through.

At the bell beginning the 13th round, Conn brashly moved in close and widened his stance. He was ready to slug it out. For the next three minutes, Conn and Louis stood toe-to-toe, swinging with

Louis zeroes in on Lou Nova during their title bout in September 1941. "From the symbol of Joe Louis' strength Negroes took strength," said the author Richard Wright, "and in that moment all fear, all obstacles were wiped out, drowned."

everything they had, giving the sport of boxing its greatest single round. In a savage exchange, with Conn's blows raining in, Louis landed a right cross to the head. Conn staggered; Louis's moment had come. Throwing every punch he knew, Louis battered Conn unmercifully. "So Joe hit me again and again, and when I finally did fall, it was a slow, funny fall. I remember that," Conn said.

The last blow was a fearful right cross to the jaw that caused Conn to double over at the waist, then pitch forward onto the canvas. Louis walked to the neutral corner taking one long, slow, deep breath as he did. With only two seconds remaining in the round, Conn was counted out.

Louis fought once more in 1941. On September 29, he met Lou Nova, an eccentric Californian who practiced yoga and bragged about his "cosmic punch." All along, Louis suspected it was a "comic punch," and he was right. Nova did little damage, and in the sixth round Louis knocked him out.

In December 1941, the champion was in Chicago, doing his best to repair his marriage. Earlier in the year, Marva had filed for divorce. She had had it with her husband's roughneck friends, his never being home, his continuous affairs with other women. Shocked by the divorce action, Joe promised to mend his ways, and Marva withdrew her petition. For a time, they had a happy second honeymoon at their Spring Hill horse farm and their Chicago apartment. Then, on Sunday afternoon, December 7, 1941, came the bulletin that rocked the Louises just as surely as it shattered the calm of every other American household: The Japanese had attacked the American fleet at Pearl Harbor, Hawaii. The United States was at war. ❧

7

"ON GOD'S SIDE"

AN ANGRY PATRIOTIC fervor swept the country in the days following Pearl Harbor. Like everyone else, Joe Louis was seething: "I couldn't even imagine anyone attacking the United States of America. I was mad, I was furious, you name it." He was ready to do his part.

The patriotic spirit captured even old Mike Jacobs. A few days after the United States went to war, Louis was playing golf at the Hillcrest Country Club in Los Angeles. Not long into his round, a caddie raced up to the champion and told him Jacobs was on the phone. It was urgent: The promoter wanted Louis to fight—for nothing.

Jacobs had the idea that Louis's purse and his own profits should go to the Navy Relief Society, a charity that looked after the families of sailors killed in action. Without hesitating, Louis said yes. Jacobs repeated the terms: a title fight for no money. "I told Mike what I'd told him before, that was fine with me," Louis recalled. Jacobs quickly scheduled a rematch with big Buddy Baer for January 9, 1942, in Madison Square Garden.

Louis's response was a wonderful gesture, absolutely unprecedented. Jack Dempsey once said, "When you're fighting, you're fighting for one thing: Money." Yet here was Louis risking his title—indeed, his livelihood and future—for nothing save the satisfaction of helping a good cause. It won for him the nation's acclaim. Columnists and sportswriters praised the champion to the hilt. Louis, wrote Bob Considine, "has hung up a mark in generosity and

Major General Irving Phillipson (right), on behalf of the Army Relief Fund, a charity to aid the families of soldiers killed in action, accepts a check worth $36,146 from Louis following his March 1942 bout against Abe Simon. Shortly after the United States entered World War II, boxing promoter Mike Jacobs (center) arranged for Louis to give his share of the purse for each title fight to a wartime charity.

93

patriotism that will not be challenged." "The more I think of it, the greater guy I see in this Joe Louis," said Jimmy Powers of the *New York Daily News*. He contrasted the champion's beneficence with the business-as-usual attitude of the industrialists supplying the armed forces: "You don't see a shipyard owner risking his entire business. If the government wants a battleship, the government doesn't ask him to donate it. The government pays him a fat profit."

It was not as though Louis did not need the money. Despite the fat purses from the Conn and Nova fights ($152,905 and $199,500, respectively) Louis was in financial hot water. He continued spending as if there were no tomorrow, among other things playing golf for stakes as high as $1,000 a hole and buying for Marva a classic Duesenberg roadster. Several investments had gone bad, and he owed Jacobs $59,000 and Roxborough $41,000. Worse, a steep tax bill was coming due early in 1942.

Yet Louis did not even consider going back on his pledge to Navy Relief. Asked repeatedly by reporters how it felt to be fighting for nothing, he finally snorted, "Ain't fighting for nothing. I'm fighting for my country."

On January 9, 1942, 17,000 people filed into flag-bedecked Madison Square Garden. It was a gala occasion. Prior to the opening bell, Wendell Willkie, the Republican nominee for president in 1940, paid tribute to Louis's "magnificent example" of patriotic sacrifice.

In his dressing room, the champion was more concerned about Jack Blackburn than about Buddy Baer, the navy, or Wendell Willkie. The trainer's health was not the best. At training camp, he had turned over most of his duties to assistant trainer Mannie Seamon. And now, moments before they were to head for the ring, Blackburn told Louis he could not make it. "My heart's bad. I don't think I can make those stairs tonight," he said to his fighter.

"You got to," pleaded Louis. Blackburn had been in his corner for every fight, and Louis could not imagine going on without him. "If you get up those stairs with me, I'll have Baer out before you can relax."

"OK," agreed Blackburn, "and remember, that's a promise."

"The only way I could have beaten Joe that night was with a baseball bat," Baer said. Louis made good on his promise to Blackburn. In the first round, he floored Baer 3 times and flattened him for good at 2 minutes, 56 seconds.

The next day, January 10, 1942, Louis volunteered for service in the United States Army. It was not the ordinary enlistment. Reporters and photographers followed his every move through the physical examination and induction. The army, unsurprisingly, found him physically fit, and the newsreel camera caught the moment when a self-conscious soldier at a typewriter asked Louis for his occupation. "Fighting and let us at them [Japanese]," the champion replied.

Louis did not have to volunteer. He had registered for the draft in 1940 and could have waited to be conscripted, or he could have claimed an exemption, being the sole support of his wife and mother. Neither road appealed to him. "Marva was living like a queen," he explained. "I mean what could I say? 'I have to be exempted so I can work so that my wife can pay the housekeeper!'"

The heavyweight champion of the world was not just another GI. After his induction, the army decided that it would be a nice thing if Private Joe Louis fought for the army's relief fund, as he had done for the navy's. Louis was happy to once more forgo a purse, and Jacobs arranged a rematch with another member of the Bum of the Month Club, 260-pound Abe Simon. In March 1941, at Detroit, Louis had knocked Simon out, but not until the 13th round.

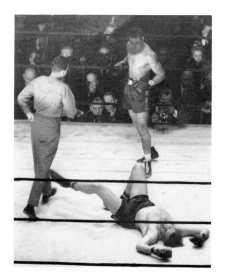

Buddy Baer lies on the canvas at Madison Square Garden on January 9, 1942, after Louis knocked him out in 2 minutes, 56 seconds of the first round. Louis's already lofty reputation soared even more when he volunteered for the U.S. Army the following day to help with the nation's war effort.

Their fight for Army Relief was scheduled for March 27, 1942, at Madison Square Garden.

The army accommodated Louis by stationing him at Fort Dix, New Jersey, not far from New York, and relieving him from all but a couple of hours a day of soldiering. At Fort Dix, he arose at six every morning and did several miles of roadwork. At 10:30 A.M., in uniform, he drilled and marched with the other troops. By early afternoon, he had resumed training in the camp gymnasium. There, as many as 2,000 GIs elbowed their way into the stands to watch the champion box with his sparring partners. By 10:00 P.M., he was in bed.

On March 10, Louis broke this routine to attend a banquet and rally for the Navy Relief Society at Madison Square Garden. That afternoon, he dropped by Jacobs's office, where Harry Markson, Jacobs's publicist, drew him aside for a caution about the banquet. "You know, Joe," he said, "they're probably going to ask you to make a speech. Do you want me to write something for you?"

"Aaahh, they're not gonna call on me," Louis said.

"What if they ask you to talk?"

"Nah, they won't ask me."

Of course they did. Private Louis, who would rather have fought Schmeling again than make a public speech, concealed his nervousness and glided to the microphone. He said what he meant: "I have only done what any red-blooded American would do." The audience applauded. "We gonna do our part, and we will win, because we are on God's side. Thank you." The audience roared.

With those few, rather trite words, Louis scored as clean a knockout as any in the ring. President Roosevelt sent a message of thanks, and the *Saturday Evening Post*, reminding its readers of the gruesome enemies the nation faced in Japan and Nazi Germany, ran a poem entitled "Joe Louis Named the War."

A World War II poster features Louis and the brief speech he made in early 1942 at a ceremonial dinner and rally for a wartime charity, the Navy Defense Fund.

Pvt. Joe Louis says_

"We're going to do our part ...and we'll win because we're on God's side"

For the second fight with Abe Simon, Louis had a particularly enthusiastic cheering section in the Garden. When he found out that some of his black friends in the army could not afford tickets, he reached into his pocket for $3,000 and bought them seats. They saw what they had come to see—another Louis knockout. Both fighters started slowly; a minute and a half went by before either threw a serious punch. Louis soon warmed to his task, dropping the massive Simon to the canvas in the second and fifth rounds. At the start of the sixth, Louis struck with a left-right combination that ended the fight. Don Dunphy, broadcasting on Mutual, said Louis symbolized the American resolve to win the war: "We won't stop punching, just as Louis does, till we win."

Louis with his trainer—and surrogate father—Jack Blackburn. "You got to listen to everything I tell you," the former boxer told Louis at the beginning of their relationship. "You got to jump when I say jump, sleep when I say sleep. Other than that, you're wasting my time."

That night, Jack Blackburn was not in the champion's corner but in a Chicago hospital, dying. "Keep punchin', Chappie," Louis said over the radio during his postfight interview. The army granted him a five-day furlough to visit the trainer's bedside. With Louis around, coming by each day to talk and joke about their shared triumphs, Blackburn got a little better. But when his fighter returned to the army, Blackburn suffered a fatal heart attack. Receiving the news, Louis broke down and sobbed. He had lost the man who had been to him a father, teacher, and friend. "He made a fighter of me and did more for me than anyone else," he said sadly.

John Roxborough, too, was no longer around. Along with 88 policemen and a former mayor of Detroit, he had been done in by a wave of reform that had smashed the Detroit numbers racket. Convicted for his prominent part in the operation, he began in 1943 serving a two-and-a-half-year stretch in a Michigan penitentiary. In his cell, over the radio, he placed a sign reading Don't Give Up Hope.

With Blackburn dead, Roxborough behind bars, and Marva still feeling neglected, Louis became more self-reliant than ever before. "When I didn't have them around to think for me and tell me what to eat and when to go to bed, I had to figure things out myself," he said. "I grew up in the Army."

Nothing, however, had happened to Mike Jacobs. He had recovered from the dose of patriotism he had taken after Pearl Harbor: According to one high government official, the promoter never got around to donating his share of the proceeds from the Baer fight to Navy Relief. He nevertheless liked the *idea* of fights for charity—it was good public relations—and in September 1942 he proposed to the army a blockbuster that would fill any stadium in the country: Louis against Billy Conn.

This time the promoter attached some strings. Jacobs, of course, controlled the 2 fighters, and both owed him considerable amounts: Louis, around $60,000; Conn, nearly $35,000. Jacobs wanted his money back, so he suggested to the army that Louis and Conn keep just enough of the gate to pay off their debts. Furthermore, he demanded control of the first 20 rows of seats, something an old scalper like Jacobs could parlay into a small fortune. Even with all this skimmed off the top, there would have been a goodly amount left for Army Relief, around $750,000.

Louis and Conn started training. Boxing fans dreamed of a donnybrook as wonderful as their first go-round. And then the army called the whole thing off. The civilian head of the army, Secretary of War Henry L. Stimson, smelled a rat. Careful to criticize neither fighter, Stimson said it would be unfair for a soldier to work off a private debt while serving his country. In truth, he did not trust Mike Jacobs and was appalled by his request for 20 rows of seats. Stimson went on to ban all future fights for military charities, saying they had more than enough money.

For Louis, the decision meant that as long as he was in uniform he would have no way of getting out of debt. By the fall of 1942, he owed Jacobs, Rox-borough, and the government more than $200,000.

As it turned out, a Louis-Conn fight would never have come off as scheduled. During his training, Conn had gone home to Pittsburgh for the christening of his son. At a party after the ceremony, he had gotten into an argument with his father-in-law. One thing led to another, and Conn let him have it with his best, a left hook. The older man ducked, and the punch landed squarely on his skull. Conn screamed. He had broken his hand. Many times thereafter, whenever Louis ran into Conn, he always asked the same thing: "Billy, is your old father-in-law still beating you up?"

Barred from title fights, Louis made the best of being one of the most famous enlisted men in the United States Army. Like more anonymous black soldiers, he served in an army that practiced racial discrimination, segregating blacks into separate units under white commanders. "Leadership is not imbedded in the Negro race yet" was Secretary Stimson's explanation.

Corporal Joe Louis trains with an all-black cavalry unit at Fort Riley, Kansas. The army assigned him to the unit after Undersecretary of War Robert Patterson learned that Louis was a lover of horses.

For a while, Louis was assigned to an all-black cavalry unit at Fort Riley, Kansas. There he met Jackie Robinson, an all-American football player from UCLA whose great fame came in another sport. In 1947, as an infielder for the Brooklyn Dodgers, he became the first black in the 20th century to play major league baseball.

Robinson idolized Louis and discovered that the champion was unafraid to use his celebrity to improve the lot of black troops. In one instance, when the applications of Robinson and some other blacks for officer candidate school (OCS) were gathering dust, Louis telephoned some influential friends in Washington, D.C. "Within a week—I say within a week, it could have been longer—we were in officer candidate school. All of the black candidates passed and became officers. It was my first experience with Louis," said Robinson.

Later, Robinson got into some serious trouble by striking a white officer who had called him a "stupid nigger." Louis hurried to the post's commanding officer, offered him a selection of expensive gifts, and, with this bribe, kept Robinson in OCS. When Robinson's unit graduated, the champion bought them all finely tailored new uniforms. It was the least he could do. "If there would be anybody I'd like to be like in this world," Louis said later, "I'd have to say it would be Jackie Robinson."

Although the army eventually promoted Louis to sergeant, it had no wish to see him fight the war in the cavalry. Rather, he was valued, as were other famous athletes, for his ability to lift the morale of the millions of American troops stationed at home and abroad.

In early 1943, Louis went to Hollywood for the filming of a flag-waving extravaganza, *This Is the Army*. Scores of stars and celebrities had roles. The heavyweight champion made a brief patriotic speech in the film and appeared as a rather uncertain participant in a lavish, all-black musical number. It was a small part, but it kept him in Hollywood for six months, and he wasted little time in rekindling his affections for several actresses.

Marva had just given birth to their first child, a baby girl they named Jacqueline. The sudden responsibility of fatherhood did not prevent Louis, however, from falling head over heels for the actress and singer Lena Horne. As the moviemaking proceeded, Louis said, "I was feeling like a dog. I wanted to marry Lena, didn't want to leave Marva, especially with my new baby." Before long, he and Horne had a fight and when he called to apologize, she hung up on him. "End of romance," said the champion.

Louis's tour of duty in Hollywood completed, the War Department decided it would be a good idea for him to lead a group of black boxers on a tour of military bases, where they could entertain the troops by staging exhibitions. Including his old sparring partner George Nicholson and a hot young welterweight from Detroit named Sugar Ray Robinson, the group of boxers came to be known as the Joe Louis Troupe. In the fall of 1943, Louis and his boxers barnstormed the country, from Alaska to Alabama. Everywhere, soldiers cheered them.

And everywhere they saw and felt the bane of racial segregation. At a camp in Virginia, black troops were given all the worst seats for the exhibition fights. Louis confronted the commanding officer. "I'm not going to box," he told the general. "You can order me to fight but I won't get in the ring." Changes were made at once, and the black troops got seats nearer the ring.

At Camp Silbert, Alabama, Louis and Sugar Ray Robinson casually sat down together on a bench in front of the post bus station. Along came a military policeman, who ordered them to the "colored" bench down the street. "That's for people like you," the man snarled.

Louis plays a duet with entertainer Lena Horne, with whom he had a brief romance. Like many black Americans, Horne admired Louis for being "the one invincible Negro, the one who stood up to the white man and beat him down with his fists."

Louis signs autographs for his fellow soldiers on the Aleutian Islands during World War II. Throughout his stint in the army, military officials asked him to boost the morale of American troops at home and abroad.

"We ain't moving," said the heavyweight champion of the world.

"Well, you're under arrest."

At the camp stockade, an officer lit into Louis and Robinson: "When an MP [military policeman] tells you to do something, you do it."

"Sir, I'm a soldier like any other American soldier. I don't want to be pushed to the back because I'm a Negro," Louis said. Accounts of the incident leaked to the press, and partly as a consequence the army eliminated segregated buses at its forts and bases.

In 1944, the Joe Louis Troupe traveled overseas to stage exhibitions for servicemen in Great Britain, Italy, and North Africa. Abroad, as at home, the champion was a GI's best friend. He answered every hard-luck story with some cash and bought a steak dinner for any soldier who could lift a knife and fork. This generosity cost dearly, particularly for a man living on borrowed money. By the end of the war, his debt to Mike Jacobs had got even larger.

Louis took off his uniform for good in October 1945, a month after World War II was officially over. During his nearly 4 years in the army, he had criss-crossed the globe, fought 96 exhibitions, visited countless hospitals, and in his quiet way had brought a moment of great good cheer into the dreary life of the American GI. Now he was a civilian once more.

And, coincidentally, a single man. In March 1945, while her husband was still in the service, Marva had obtained a divorce. "Joe thinks I ought to be happy because I've got all the material things any woman could want," she said. "But it's no fun being alone all the time."

8

"SAVE ME, JOE LOUIS"

❧

FIVE YEARS AND a day after their first meeting, Joe Louis and Billy Conn fought again. The sporting public had waited through a world war for the rematch, anticipating another battle royal.

The fight was a dud. "A stinkeroo," said Conn. By the middle rounds, some in the crowd at Yankee Stadium tired of yelling for action and started booing. Louis said he could not really blame them.

The long layoff had done neither fighter any good, but it was Conn who most visibly showed its effects, weighing in at 182, a far cry from his weight of 169 in 1941. Five years and 13 pounds had ruined most of his quickness and stamina. He was no longer fast enough to beat Louis to the punch, and for seven rounds he just tried to stay out of the champion's way. Before the eighth round, Louis told Mannie Seamon, Blackburn's successor as trainer, that he was going to turn up the pressure and see if Conn could take it. He couldn't. Louis's jab got Conn into trouble, and an overhand right caused his knees to buckle. A right uppercut followed by a left hook knocked Conn out. Minutes later, in his dressing room, Conn's trainer Johnny Ray sobbed, "Billy's finished," and, as a boxer, he was.

It was business as usual for Louis on June 19, 1946, in his first title bout after World War II: Billy Conn puts his gloves over his eyes and lies flat on his back after being kayoed by Louis's left hook.

Compared to Conn, Louis was a remarkable specimen. For the fight, he came in at a trim 207, only a few pounds over his prewar weight. Although his hair had thinned and his facial features had been softened by added flesh, he looked about the same as he had before the war. There was, however, no mistaking his age. He was 32, and at 30 a boxer is past his prime; at 35 he is old. During the Conn fight, Louis showed his years. The punches packed the same power, but his hands did not have the old quickness, and his footwork—not rapid to begin with—had slowed. As one observer cracked, the Conn rematch was "an exercise in slow motion."

The fight drew the second-largest live gate in boxing history, nearly $2 million. Louis's purse, $625,000, was the best payday of his career. Yet it was not enough to get him out of financial trouble. He had to pay his managers their cut, $140,000, out of his share. Marva sliced off $66,000 as part of their divorce settlement. He repaid Mike Jacobs and John Roxborough $200,000, and to the Internal Revenue Service went $115,000 for his taxes from 1941. After the state of New York took its share, $30,000, the champion had roughly $70,000—a considerable sum, but he had not paid a penny of federal income tax on the purse, and that enormous bill would soon be coming due.

"I made half a million dollars, and I was broke," Louis said, succinctly summing up his plight.

Another fight and another purse seemed to be the answer. In September 1946, three months after beating Conn, Louis met Tami Mauriello, a lumbering heavyweight with a mean punch and an undistinguished record. "I didn't consider him any threat at all," Louis recalled, "so I was really surprised when in the first round he shot me a right on the chin that almost threw me." The dazed champion clinched and hung on. Mauriello failed to make the most of his

Throughout Louis's life, most of his financial investments, including this restaurant in Harlem, met with little success. As a result, he had to keep on fighting so he could pay off his debts.

chance, once throwing a punch that came closer to hitting the referee than Louis.

Louis's head cleared quickly. He grabbed the offensive. His pride had been stung by Mauriello's booming punch, and he pasted his foe with a series of combinations. Mauriello was too slow to get out of harm's way, and Louis put him down twice. The second time, the referee counted him out, and Louis had another first-round knockout. It was the 23rd time he had successfully defended his title. "I had complete control, energy, power," he recalled. "I wonder sometimes if that wasn't my last great fight."

After it was over, Marshall Miles, Louis's manager while Roxborough languished in jail, attempted to bring some sense to the champion's finances. For the Mauriello fight, Louis received slightly more than $100,000. Miles told Mike Jacobs to hold the purse until January 1947, when it could be used to pay income taxes. "We'll come and get it in January of next year," he told Jacobs. "Just make sure it's all there."

In January, neither the purse nor the promoter was there. Jacobs had suffered a stroke, and while he was mending, Sol Strauss of the Twentieth Century Sporting Club had sent out checks and money orders to Louis. All Miles found in Jacobs's office was a mountain of cancelled checks and Western Union money order receipts made out to the boxer. Of the $100,000, only $500 remained.

It took Miles a while to track Louis down, but the manager eventually found him and got his side of the story. The champion rather sheepishly explained that he had put $40,000 into the Rhumboogie Cafe on Garfield Boulevard in Chicago, a sure-thing investment, and the rest had just gone—as it had always gone—on women, on the golf course, on friends, on clothes and cars. And, he added, the Rhumboogie had folded.

"Why did you leave $500 when you took all that other money?" Miles finally asked. Louis only laughed.

Meanwhile, he and Marva were back together. Their divorce had been remarkably friendly. The champion often stayed with his ex-wife and little Jacqueline, paying their bills, and, as he did every year when the new models came out, buying Marva a new car. Still in love, the couple remarried in July 1946. This time Marva knew what to expect. Her husband was simply not cut out for marital fidelity, and he shortly resumed his other romances. "He supported women around the country," recalled Leonard Reed, Louis's personal secretary. "I had a list of women I'd send money to religiously. I got them apartments and paid the rent so he could go there when he was in town."

The remarriage did nothing to ease Louis's financial bind. Marva also liked the best of everything, and, what was more, she was expecting another child. Returns from the investments Louis had made over the years would have come in very handy, but the Rhumboogie Cafe fiasco was fairly typical of his business ventures. Nightclubs and restaurants he backed went under. A cherry-flavored soft drink called Joe Louis Punch never caught on, and a deal with Sugar Ray Robinson to distribute Canadian Ace Beer collapsed.

The only place, then, for Louis to make the money he needed was in the ring. The problem was that with Conn and Mauriello beaten, there were no heavyweights of championship caliber left. So, needing cash, Louis spent the fall of 1946 and the winter and spring of 1947 on the road, fighting exhibition matches. An excursion through Central and South America drew large crowds and paid $10,000 an appearance. Not surprisingly, the champion brought along a large, lively entourage, and after he covered their expenses not much was left. There was, however, one delightful springtime dividend. On May 24, 1947, in Mexico City, Marva gave birth to a baby boy: Joe Louis Barrow, Jr.

At last, in late 1947, a championship fight was lined up. On December 5 at Madison Square Garden, Louis would meet a lightly regarded black fighter from Camden, New Jersey: Jersey Joe Walcott.

"I think I would have quit fighting if I had knocked Walcott out in an early round," Louis said later. He was not to be so fortunate. Although Walcott had a poor record, he was a fine fighter who, because he was black and poor, had never had the advantage of proper training. He had gone into the ring more than once with an empty stomach—and lost. Walcott was a man who had once earned a living cleaning cesspools, and on December 5, 1947, he was not about to let his one grand chance slip away.

Walcott came out dancing, and he kept on sprinting for 15 rounds. Louis tried to get close enough for some action, but he appeared to lack the energy to

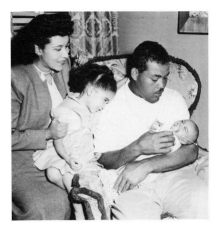

The Louis family in 1947: Joe holds his newborn son, Joe, Jr., as his first wife, Marva, and daughter, Jacqueline, look on.

trap his opponent. He seemed awkward, even clumsy. When he did get Walcott in range, his timing was off and his punches missed. In round one, the challenger stood still long enough to throw a solid right. It hit Louis's jaw and knocked him down for a two count. In the fourth round, Walcott did it again, and Louis was on his hands and knees until the count reached seven. The round passed with Walcott circling the ring and Louis in listless pursuit.

Only once, in the ninth, did Louis get Walcott where he wanted him. Trapped on the ropes, Walcott took everything the champion could muster and then fought back. "I knew my chance for a knockout was over," Louis said.

When it ended, most of the 20,000 spectators in the Garden believed they had just witnessed one of the most amazing upsets in boxing history. Walcott, after all, had knocked the champion down twice, and as Louis went to his corner after the final bell he looked beaten. Not wanting to hear the judges' decision, he tried to leave the ring, only to be restrained by his seconds.

It was a split decision: the referee for Walcott, the two judges at ringside narrowly for Louis. He had survived by the skin of his teeth. When ring announcer Harry Balogh shouted into the microphone, "The winner by majority decision and still the heavyweight champion of the world, Joe Louis," the crowd started booing. For the first time, the fans were against him. "Those boos went right to my bones," Louis recalled. "I felt a depression I had never felt before."

Later, in his New York apartment, Louis spoke over the telephone with his mother. "I thought that would have been the last fight," she said, "but I know you got to go in there and fight that boy." Those were exactly her son's sentiments. He could not end his career with the crowd booing; he would have to fight Joe Walcott again and knock him out.

Louis talks to the press in June 1948 at his Pompton Lakes, New Jersey, training site, shortly before his rematch with Jersey Joe Walcott. The two boxers first met in December 1947, with Louis winning narrowly, on a split decision. Although their second bout was not nearly as close—Louis knocked out Walcott in the 11th round—the undefeated heavyweight champion announced his intention to retire immediately after the fight.

On June 25, 1948, after two days of rain had forced two postponements of the fight, the skies over Yankee Stadium cleared, and Louis and Walcott had their return engagement. Thirteen years before, to the exact day and hour, in the same spacious ballpark, a glorious young boxer from Detroit had taken the world by storm when he demolished Primo Carnera. Now, old and tired, needing another payday and wanting to recover his reputation, Louis would be defending his title for the 25th and final time.

Walcott stayed with what had served him so well in the first fight. He circled the ring, keeping out of Louis's range. But this time the champion did not try to chase him. He waited for Walcott to come to him. In the third round, Walcott did, and Louis got the worst of it. The challenger stung him with a left-right combination that put him down. But Louis bounded to his feet before the referee could start the count.

After this flurry, the fight settled into tedium. Walcott danced around; Louis held his ground. The crowd screamed for action. Even the referee begged the fighters to mix it up.

In the 11th round, Walcott stopped moving, and Louis had his chance. With all his strength, he unleashed a barrage that drove Walcott into the ropes, then overpowered him with a series of lefts to the head. Walcott fell to the canvas, knocked out.

The 43,000 in Yankee Stadium sent up a tremendous volley of applause. It was like the glory days of old. "The cheers were for me and I loved every minute of it," Louis said. On the radio immediately after the fight, he announced his intention to retire.

On March 1, 1949, Joe Louis formally relinquished his title, the first heavyweight since Gene Tunney 20 years before not to lose the championship in the ring. His retirement was the centerpiece of an arrangement creating a new organization, the International Boxing Club (IBC). Louis was part of the IBC from the outset and had visions of replacing Mike Jacobs as boxing's premier promoter. He signed contracts with the four leading heavyweight contenders and started arranging an elimination tournament, the winner getting the vacated title. However, before his particular promotion could get going, he sold his interests to his IBC partners. He was not destined to be the new "Uncle Mike." For his title and contracts, the IBC paid Louis $350,000 and guaranteed him a yearly salary of $20,000.

The IBC staged its Tournament of Champions, and in June 1949 Ezzard Charles, a 29-year-old boxer who had once fought as a middleweight, defeated Walcott and succeeded Louis as heavyweight champion.

Louis's retirement was neither very peaceful nor very long. During the winter of 1949, Marva divorced him, this time for good. She simply could stand no more of her husband's casual attitude toward marriage. Then, in 1950, the Internal Revenue Service, after years of snooping around, completed an audit of Louis's tangled finances. The IRS bureaucrats proceeded to land a punch worse than anything Schmeling or Conn had thrown. They determined Louis owed the federal government back taxes amounting to more than $500,000. It was an impossibly large sum that the former champion had not the slightest chance of paying. Louis's lawyers dickered with the IRS and managed to knock some off the figure, but the government wanted its money and promised to make Louis's life miserable until they got it.

Louis had no choice but to put on his boxing gloves again if he wanted to make a dent of any kind in the back taxes. He had got a little bored playing so much golf, and he made the best of necessity, persuading himself he could be the first man to regain the heavyweight title. Still the most famous boxer in the world, he had no difficulty getting a match with Ezzard Charles, the new champion. But because the bout was arranged on short notice, he had only 6 weeks to train, not long enough for someone 36 years old who had been inactive for 2 years. On September 27, 1950, the day of the fight, he weighed in at a much too heavy 218 pounds.

Ezzard Charles was a methodical, precise boxer who lacked punching power. If he had had a knockout punch, his fight with Louis might have ended quickly. As it was, the small crowd of 13,000 at Yankee Stadium and the 20 million watching on television saw 15 long, painful rounds of Joe Louis being pushed all over the ring. Darting in and out, Charles hit Louis almost at will. Louis was too slow and weary to do anything about it. Bruised and bleeding, he had to be lifted off his stool at the beginning of the final round.

The unanimous decision went to Charles. For only the second time, Louis had lost a professional fight. One of his eyes had swollen tightly shut, and in his dressing room he could not see well enough to put on his trousers. His good friend Sugar Ray Robinson helped him on with his shoes and, with some others, led him from the stadium.

Beating the greatest heavyweight in history should have been Ezzard Charles's brightest moment.

The end of an era: Rocky Marciano (right) sends the 37-year-old Louis to the canvas (opposite) and back into retirement. The bout, which took place at Madison Square Garden on October 26, 1951, was Louis's last fight—but not his last appearance in the ring.

It was anything but. When he returned to his home in Cincinnati, black youngsters hooted at him, furious at the black man who had conquered Louis. "Louis was proof that a Negro could escape the slums," wrote Jimmy Cannon of the feelings in the black ghetto. "They yearned for him to last forever. It made them ache because he could be defeated. It didn't matter that Charles was black. He had beaten Louis, and they would not forgive him. He had stolen something from their lives."

Louis's purse amounted to about $30,000, far less than anticipated. The IRS was getting impatient. "The government wanted their money and I had to try and get it to them," Louis said, meaning, of course, more fights. Between November 1950 and May 1951, he fought five times. His opponents were, to put it charitably, mediocre. A boxer like Charles was too much for him to handle, but against second- and third-stringers Louis could—and did—win easily.

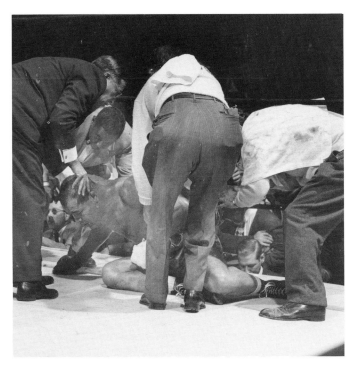

In June 1951, Louis knocked out a better fighter, Lee Savold, the heavyweight champion of the British Empire. Once more there was hopeful talk of his regaining the championship. "I convinced myself I could still get it," he said. "I wanted the money it would bring, and I don't mind saying now that I wanted the cheers, too."

The hope and cheers died in Madison Square Garden on October 26, 1951, the victims of a 28-year-old heavyweight from Brockton, Massachusetts: Rocky Marciano. Within a year, Marciano would win the title, and within five he would retire undefeated. But during the beginning rounds in the Garden that evening, Louis outfought Marciano, using his jab to keep the younger man off balance. In the sixth, however, his legs betrayed him, and Marciano took control.

In the eighth, Marciano administered a terrible beating. "Right after Marciano knocked Louis down the first time," wrote A. J. Leibling in the *New*

Yorker, "Sugar Ray Robinson started working his way toward the ring, as if drawn by some horrid fascination, and by the time Rocky threw the final right, Robinson's hand was on the lowest rope of the ring, as if he meant to jump in. The punch knocked Joe through the ropes and he lay on the ring apron, only one leg inside."

Louis knew he was finished as a fighter: "I looked at myself and wondered what the hell I was going to do now?"

One thing Louis did not do was feel sorry for himself. He left boxing broke, but he had no regrets. Through the years, he heard over and over from many people what a shame it was he had never got a shot at the large, inflated boxing purses of the 1960s and 1970s. "No," Louis would say, "when I was boxing I made five million dollars and wound up broke, owing the government a million. If I was boxing today I'd make ten million and wind up broke, owing the government two million."

The million dollars was no exaggeration. In 1956, IRS agents sharpened their pencils and recalculated Louis's tax liability. Counting interest and penalties, they came up with $1,200,000. It might as well have been $10 million or $100 million. The only stable income Louis had was the $20,000 a year from the IBC.

The government took what it could. When his mother died in 1953, Louis said, "There was nothing I could do but cry." And, he might have added, curse Uncle Sam. The IRS seized the $667 Lillie Barrow Brooks left her son. He and Marva had set up trust funds for their two children. The IRS grabbed that money as well. Eventually, the government agreed to limit its collection of back taxes to $20,000 a year, exactly what Louis was getting from the IBC. "I must have been earning about $33,000," he recalled, "and when I paid $12,000 tax on the $33,000, plus the

$20,000, I'd only have $1,000 left. You know, something like that can depress a man."

Louis did what he could to make a buck. He refereed fights. He endorsed products. He dabbled in advertising and public relations. And, in a move that caused his friends and loved ones to wince, he went on tour as a professional wrestler. "It was like seeing the President of the United States washing dishes," said one observer.

Louis's time in the "sport" was limited. During one match, Cowboy Rocky Lee, a 320-pound competitor, accidentally stepped on Louis's chest, breaking 2 ribs and damaging the muscles around the heart. The injuries ended his career as a wrestler.

Despite the problems with money, Louis lived well, if not in the grand style of his days as champion. He had friends everywhere. Strangers shouted "Hi, Champ" the moment they saw him; entertainers begged him to join their golfing foursomes, and later at dinner it was they, not he, who reached for the check. Women still found him irresistible. On Christmas Day, 1955, he married Rose Morgan, a stunning cosmetics and beauty expert from Harlem. "We lasted

In 1956, Louis went on tour as a professional wrestler. His new-found career ended a few matches later, however, when one of his opponents landed on Louis's chest, breaking two ribs and damaging the muscles around his heart.

Louis with his third wife, Martha Malone Jefferson. They were married in 1959.

about six weeks," Louis confessed. It was the same old story. "I tried to make him settle down," Rose said. "I told him he couldn't sleep all day and stay out all night any more." Her luck was no different from Marva's, and in 1958 the marriage was annulled.

Not long afterward, Louis met Martha Malone Jefferson, an independent, forthright woman different from his earlier loves. A prosperous attorney, she had been the first black woman admitted to the California bar, and before meeting Louis she had never known a prizefighter. She did not fall for his money or good looks. By the time they met, he was broke, balding, and overweight. "There's a soul about this man, and a quietness that I love," she explained. They married in 1959, and he moved into her spacious Los Angeles home.

Martha brought a certain order to Louis's life—he called her "sergeant"—but she did not try to remake him. She tolerated his trips to New York for matters other than business and did not object to his daily rounds of golf. At home, she placed a television in nearly every room. Even his bathroom had a set so the former champion would not miss a show while taking a shower. "Television and golf," she said in 1962, "that's Joe Louis today."

Horribly, during the 1960s, drugs also became a diversion. On one of Louis's trips to New York, an actress introduced him to cocaine. He was hooked. "It made me feel like myself just after the Carnera fight, just like after the Braddock fight, when I became the heavyweight champion of the world, like just after I won the second Schmeling fight," he said. "I kept telling myself that nothing could be wrong with feeling that good."

Nothing except nearly killing himself and losing his mind. In June 1969, Louis collapsed with severe abdominal pain, the result of a drug overdose. The emergency room of a New York hospital saved him.

But no hospital could rescue Louis from the delusions in his head. The Mafia was after him, or so he pathetically believed. They were trying to poison his food. They wanted to kill him with lethal gas. His paranoia was such that he refused the "tainted" food Martha prepared. He taped up air-conditioning ducts and smeared mayonnaise over cracks in the ceiling to stop the imaginary gas from seeping through. To protect himself from demons who were sure to catch him sleeping, he regularly made a tent out of his mattress and box spring and then would spend the night cowering underneath it.

In 1970, Louis's wife and son, both of them heartsick, committed him for a time to a psychiatric institution. He recovered, but not completely. Out of the blue, he would let loose every now and then with some angry, paranoid outburst, shocking those around him.

During the 1970s, Louis found a professional niche of sorts in Las Vegas, Nevada, America's gambling capital, where Caesar's Palace Hotel and Casino

Louis, at age 62, in Caesar's Palace Casino, the Las Vegas gaming hall where he worked as an official greeter.

A man of tremendous dignity, Louis scaled the barriers of racial segregation by showing the nation that blacks could rise to great heights when given the chance. "Prejudice is weakening. The good people are softening it up," he said. "So we can't stop punching now. We just have to punch faster and harder. That's the only way we can make America a better place for my little boy and girl and all the little boys and girls in our country."

employed him as a professional greeter. In the afternoon, he played golf with the high rollers and celebrities. In the evenings, he cruised the casino, placing bets with the house's money, glad-handing the patrons, listening for the millionth time to some well-meaning tourist gush, "I'll never forget the night you fought . . ."

In October 1977, Louis suffered a heart attack, followed by a cerebral hemorrhage. He returned to Caesar's Palace in a wheelchair that he would never be able to leave. "There are certain things you should never see," wrote sports columnist Jim Murray. "A great stage beauty in the morning without her makeup. A stag dying in the sunset. A great ship sinking. A great warrior succumbing to great odds. A lion wounded and at bay to the jackals. And Joe Louis in a wheelchair."

On Friday night, April 11, 1981, Louis was wheeled into the sports pavilion at Caesar's Palace to see a heavyweight fight. As he rolled in, every eye followed him, and then the house rose and gave him a long cheer. The following morning at 9:45, boxing's great champion, age 67, died of a heart attack. His body was buried at Arlington National Cemetery in Arlington, Virginia, 10 days later.

He had meant so much to so many. Years earlier, Martin Luther King, Jr., told the story of the southern state that had introduced the gas chamber as its means of capital punishment. State officials wanted to hear the last words of the first man executed by the gas, so they placed a microphone inside the death chamber. "The first victim was a young Negro," King said. "As the pellet dropped into the container, and gas curled upward, through the microphone came these words: 'Save me, Joe Louis. Save me, Joe Louis. Save me, Joe Louis . . .' " ✠

APPENDIX:
PROFESSIONAL FIGHT RECORD

————— ❦ —————

Date	Opponent	Result	Round
1934			
July 4	Jack Kracken	Won (by KO)	1
July 11	Willie Davis	Won (by KO)	3
July 29	Larry Udell	Won (by KO)	2
August 13	Jack Kranz	Won	8
August 27	Buck Everett	Won (by KO)	2
September 11	Alex Borchuk	Won (by KO)	4
September 25	Adolph Wiater	Won	10
October 24	Art Sykes	Won (by KO)	8
October 30	Jack O'Dowd	Won (by KO)	2
November 14	Stanley Poreda	Won (by KO)	1
November 30	Charlie Massera	Won (by KO)	3
December 14	Lee Ramage	Won (by KO)	8
1935			
January 4	Patsy Perroni	Won	10
January 11	Hans Birkie	Won (by KO)	10
February 21	Lee Ramage	Won (by KO)	2
March 8	Donald Barry	Won (by KO)	3
March 28	Natie Brown	Won	10
April 12	Roy Lazer	Won (by KO)	3
April 22	Biff Benton	Won (by KO)	2
April 27	Roscoe Toles	Won (by KO)	6
May 3	Willie Davis	Won (by KO)	2
May 7	Gene Stanton	Won (by KO)	3
June 25	Primo Carnera	Won (by KO)	6
August 7	King Levinsky	Won (by KO)	1
September 24	Max Baer	Won (by KO)	4
December 13	Paolino Uzcudun	Won (by KO)	4
1936			
January 17	Charley Retzlaff	Won (by KO)	1
June 19	Max Schmeling	Lost (by KO)	12
August 18	Jack Sharkey	Won (by KO)	3
September 22	Al Ettore	Won (by KO)	5
October 9	Jorge Brescia	Won (by KO)	3
December 14	Eddie Simms	Won (by KO)	1
1937			
January 11	Steve Ketchel	Won (by KO)	2
January 29	Bob Pastor	Won	10
February 17	Natie Brown	Won (by KO)	4
June 22	James J. Braddock	Won (by KO)	8
August 30	Tommy Farr	Won	15
1938			
February 23	Nathan Mann	Won (by KO)	3
April 1	Harry Thomas	Won (by KO)	5
June 22	Max Schmeling	Won (by KO)	1

Date	Opponent	Result	Round
1939			
January 25	John Henry Lewis	Won (by KO)	1
April 17	Jack Roper	Won (by KO)	1
June 28	Tony Galento	Won (by KO)	4
September 20	Bob Pastor	Won (by KO)	11
1940			
February 9	Arturo Godoy	Won	15
March 29	Johnny Paycheck	Won (by KO)	2
June 20	Arturo Godoy	Won (by KO)	8
December 16	Al McCoy	Won (by KO)	1
1941			
January 31	Red Burman	Won (by KO)	5
February 17	Gus Dorazio	Won (by KO)	2
March 21	Abe Simon	Won (by KO)	13
April 8	Tony Musto	Won (by KO)	9
May 23	Buddy Baer	Won	7
June 18	Billy Conn	Won (by KO)	13
September 29	Lou Nova	Won (by KO)	6
1942			
January 9	Buddy Baer	Won (by KO)	1
March 27	Abe Simon	Won (by KO)	6
1946			
June 19	Billy Conn	Won (by KO)	8
September 18	Tami Mauriello	Won (by KO)	1
1947			
December 5	Jersey Joe Walcott	Won	15
1948			
June 25	Jersey Joe Walcott	Won (by KO)	11
1950			
September 27	Ezzard Charles	Lost	15
November 29	Cesar Brion	Won	10
1951			
January 3	Freddie Beshore	Won (by KO)	4
February 7	Omelio Agramonte	Won	10
February 23	Andy Walker	Won (by KO)	10
May 2	Omelio Agramonte	Won	10
June 15	Lee Savold	Won (by KO)	6
August 1	Cesar Brion	Won	10
August 15	Jimmy Bivins	Won	10
October 26	Rocky Marciano	Lost (by KO)	8

(Overall Record: 68–3)

CHRONOLOGY

1914   Born Joe Louis Barrow on May 13 near Lafayette, Alabama

1926   Moves to Detroit, Michigan

1932   Loses his first amateur fight

1934   Wins the Detroit Golden Gloves and the Amateur Athletic Union light-heavy-weight titles; moves to Chicago, Illinois, to train with Jack Blackburn; wins his first professional fight by beating Jack Kracken in the first round on July 4

1935   Beats Primo Carnera in six rounds on June 25; marries Marva Trotter and beats Max Baer in four rounds on September 24

1936   Appears in the film *The Spirit of Youth*; loses to Max Schmeling in 12 rounds on June 19

1937   Beats James Braddock in eight rounds on June 22 to win the heavyweight title

1938   Beats Schmeling in first round on June 22

1939   Beats John Henry Lewis in first round on January 25

1941   Beats Billy Conn in 13 rounds on June 18

1942   Volunteers for the U.S. Army

1943   First child, Jacqueline, is born

1945   First marriage ends in divorce; Louis is discharged from the army

1946   Remarries Marva Trotter

1947   Second child, Joe Louis Barrow, Jr., is born; Louis beats Joe Walcott by a split decision on December 5

1948   Beats Joe Walcott in 11 rounds on June 25

1949   Formally relinquishes the heavyweight title on March 1; second marriage ends in divorce

1950   Louis is audited by Internal Revenue Service; loses to Ezzard Charles in 15 rounds on September 27

1951   Loses to Rocky Marciano in eight rounds on October 26

1955   Marries Rose Morgan

1956   Becomes a professional wrestler

1958   Third marriage is annulled

1959   Louis marries Martha Malone Jefferson

1981   Dies on April 12 in Las Vegas, Nevada

FURTHER READING

Andre, Sam, and Nat Fleisher. *A Pictorial History of Boxing.* New York: Bonanza Books, 1981.

Astor, Gerald. *". . . And a Credit to His Race": The Hard Life and Times of Joseph Louis Barrow, a.k.a. Joe Louis.* New York: Dutton, 1974.

Barrow, Joe L., Jr., and Barbara Munder. *Joe Louis: Fifty Years an American Hero.* New York: McGraw-Hill, 1988.

Blum, John Morton. *V Was for Victory.* New York: Harcourt Brace Jovanovich, 1976.

Davis, Lenwood G. *Joe Louis: A Bibliography of Articles, Books, Pamphlets, Records, & Archival Materials.* Westport, CT: Greenwood, 1983.

Edmonds, A. O. *Joe Louis.* Grand Rapids, MI: Eerdmans, 1973.

Libby, Bill. *Joe Louis: The Brown Bomber.* New York: Lothrop, 1980.

Louis, Joe, Jr., and Art Rust. *Joe Louis: My Life.* New York: Berkley, 1981.

Mead, Chris. *Champion: Joe Louis.* New York: Scribners, 1985.

———. *Champion: Joe Louis: Black Hero in White America.* New York: Penguin, 1986.

Miller, Margery. *Joe Louis: American.* New York: Current Books, 1945.

Nagler, Barney. *Brown Bomber.* New York: World Publishing, 1972.

Sugar, Bert Randolph. *The Ring Record Book and Boxing Encyclopedia.* New York: Ring Publishing, 1981.

INDEX

Adams, Caswell, 58
Africa, 103
Alabama, 17, 18, 27, 29, 31, 33, 34, 101
Alaska, 101
Amateur Athletic Union (AAU), 41, 44
Arlington, Virginia, 121
Arlington National Cemetery, 121
Army Relief Fund, 95–96, 98
Austria, 16

Bacon Casino, 48
Baer, Buddy, 86–87, 88, 93, 94–95, 98
Baer, Max, 14, 20, 65, 67–68, 70, 75, 86
Balogh, Harry, 22, 23, 25, 110
Barrow, Eulalia (sister), 29
Barrow, Jacqueline Louis (daughter), 101, 108
Barrow, Joe Louis. See Louis, Joe
Barrow, Joe Louis, Jr. (son), 109
Barrow, Lillie Reese (mother), 27–30, 31–32, 34, 36, 70, 72, 110, 116
Barrow, Munroe (father), 27, 30
Berchtesgaden, Germany, 14, 22
Black, Julian, 44–45, 46, 53, 58, 66, 80, 82
Blackburn, Jack, 19, 21, 45–48, 49, 52, 53, 54, 61, 71, 74, 81, 86, 89, 94, 97, 98, 105
Borchuk, Alex, 49
Boston, Massachusetts, 41
Braddock, James J., 13, 20, 65–66, 69, 73, 74, 75–77, 82, 88, 119

Bremen, SS, 17
Brewster Recreational Center, 36, 39, 40, 43
Briggs Motor Company, 37
Brockton, Massachusetts, 115
Bronson Trade School, 34, 35–36
Brooklyn Dodgers, 100
Brooks, Pat (stepfather), 30–32 53
Brown, Nattie, 58
Buick Motor Company, 67
Burman, Red, 86

Caesar's Palace Hotel and Casino, 119–20
Camden, New Jersey, 109
Camp Hill, Alabama, 31
Camp Sibert, Alabama, 101
Canadian Ace Beer, 109
Cannon, Jimmy, 114
Capone, Al, 61
Carnera, Primo, 59–61, 62, 63, 65, 111, 119
Charles, Ezzard, 112, 113–14
Chicago, Illinois, 13, 41, 44–45, 48, 49, 54, 57, 65, 66, 70, 75, 91, 97, 108
Chicago Stadium, 53
Cincinnati, Ohio, 114
Cleveland, Ohio, 44, 74
Comiskey Park, Chicago, 13, 75, 76
Commodore Hotel, 13
Conn, Billy, 87–91, 94, 98, 99, 105–6, 109, 112
Considine, Bob, 93
Corum Bill, 79
Czechoslovakia, 16

Davis, Willie, 48
Dearborn, Michigan, 18
Dempsey, Jack, 20, 36, 61, 82
Detroit, Michigan, 32–34, 39,

41, 42–43, 44, 49, 53, 55, 58, 63, 66, 70, 81, 97–98, 101, 110
Donovan, Arthur, 23, 24, 25, 61, 85
Dorazio, Gus, 86
Duffield Elementary School, 33–34
Dunphy, Don, 88, 97

Ethiopia, 60
Evans, Stanley, 41–42

Fleischer, Nat, 86
Ford, Henry, 33
Ford Motor Company, 18, 33, 34, 40
Fort Dix, New Jersey, 96
Fort Riley, Kansas, 100
Franklin, Bonnie, 35
Free Milk Fund for Babies, 56

Galento, Tony, 83–85, 88
Germany, 14–18, 22, 75, 79, 80
Godoy, Arturo, 85–86
Gould, Joe, 75–77, 82
Great Britain, 103
Great Depression, 34, 56
Guinyard, Freddie, 34–35, 54, 72

Harlem, New York City, 14, 19, 59, 60, 66, 68, 73, 117
Havana, Cuba, 52
Hearst, William Randolph, 55, 56, 58, 81
Helmers, Arno, 22
Herald Tribune, 58, 79
Hillcrest Country Club, 93
Hindenburg, 16
Hitler, Adolf, 14–17, 19, 20, 22, 74
Hollywood, California, 100–101

Hope, Bob, 20, 22
Horne, Lena, 101

Internal Revenue Service
    (IRS), 81, 106, 112–13,
    114, 116
International Boxing Club
    (IBC), 112, 116
Italy, 103

Jacobs, Mike, 54–59, 63, 65,
    67, 69, 73, 74–75, 81–82,
    87, 88, 93, 94, 96, 98, 99,
    106, 107–8, 112
Japan, 91, 97
Jefferson, Martha Malone, 118,
    119
"Joe Louis Named the War,"
    97
Joe Louis Punch, 109
Joe Louis Troupe, 101, 103
Johnson, Jack, 13, 51–53, 63,
    66, 70
Johnston, Jimmy, 54, 55, 57,
    69, 73, 74, 75, 81

King, Martin Luther, Jr., 121
Ku Klux Klan, 31–32

Lafayette, Alabama, 27
La Guardia, Fiorello, 59
Lakewood, New Jersey, 71
Las Vegas, Nevada, 119
Lee, Cowboy Rocky, 117
Leibling, A. J., 115
Levinsky, King, 65
Lewis, John Henry, 83
Los Angeles, California, 40,
    57, 93, 118
Louis, Joe
    begins training with Jack
        Blackburn, 47
    birth, 27
    and "Bum of the Month
        Club," 79–87
    Carnera fight, 60–61
    change in name, 39–40

Charles fight, 113
death, 121
drug addiction, 119
early years, 27–37
education, 31, 33–34
financial problems, 94, 98–
    99, 103, 106, 107–9,
    112–13, 114, 116–17
first amateur fight, 39–40
first Conn fight, 87–91
first professional fight, 48
first Schmeling fight, 12, 72
forms Brown Bombers softball
    team, 70
and Joe Louis Troupe, 101,
    103
joins U.S. Army, 95
Marciano fight, 115–16
and marriage, 66–67, 103,
    112, 117, 118
Max Baer fight, 67–68
meets John Roxborough, 42
moves to Detroit, 32
as a professional wrestler, 117
purchases Spring Hill home,
    81
and racial prejudice, 31, 62–
    63, 99–100, 101
relinquishes heavyweight
    title, 112
second Schmeling fight, 23–
    25, 79
signs contract with Twen-
    tieth Century Sporting
    Club, 59
takes up boxing, 36
wins AAU title, 44
wins Detroit Golden Gloves
    title, 42
wins heavyweight title, 76–
    77
works in Las Vegas, 119
Lunt, Alfred, 87

McCarthy, Clem, 22, 24, 25,
    68, 80
McCoy, Al, 86

McKinney, Thurston, 36, 43,
    54
Madison Square Garden, 11,
    13, 19, 54, 55, 56, 57, 69,
    73, 74, 75, 81, 83, 93, 94,
    96, 97, 109, 110, 115
Marciano, Rocky, 115–16
Marek, Max, 41
Markson, Harry, 96
Massera, Charlie, 53
Mauriello, Tami, 106–7, 109
Mexico City, 109
Miler, Johnny, 40
Miles, Marshall, 107–8
Mississippi, 80
Morgan, Rose, 117–18
Mt. Sinai Baptist Church, 29–
    30, 31, 32
Murray, Jim, 120
Mussolini, Benito, 60
Musto, Tony, 86
Mutual Radio Network, 88, 97

Nagler, Barney, 85
Navy Relief Society, 93, 94,
    96, 98
Nazi Germany, 14–18, 75, 80,
    97
New Jersey, 51, 83
New York Athletic Commis-
    sion, 14
New York City, 11, 17, 18, 19,
    52, 54, 58, 59, 67, 79, 87,
    110, 118, 119
New York *Daily News*, 94
New York Hippodrome, 57
Nicholson, George, 18–19, 76,
    101
Nova, Lou, 91, 94

O'Brien, Jack, 63
Ondra, Anny, 16

Pastor, Bob, 74
Pearl Harbor, 91, 93, 98
Pennsylvania Station, 52
Pittsburgh, Pennsylvania, 87, 99

Polo Grounds, New York City, 87

Pompton Lakes, New Jersey, 18–19

Powers, Jimmy, 94

Ramage, Lee, 53, 57

Ramapo Mountains, 18

Ray, Johnny, 87, 88, 89, 105

Reed, Leonard, 108

Rhumboogie Cafe, 108, 109

Rice, Grantland, 23

Rickard, Tex, 55

Ring magazine, 36, 85

Robinson, Jackie, 100

Robinson, Sugar Ray, 101–2, 109, 113, 115

Roosevelt, Eleanor, 81

Roosevelt, Franklin D., 18, 96

Roxborough, John, 42–45, 46, 52, 53, 54, 57, 58, 80, 82, 94, 97, 99, 106, 107

Runyon, Damon, 56, 61

Ruth, Babe, 22

Saturday Evening Post, 97

Savold, Lee, 114

Schmeling, Max, 12–14, 15–25, 69, 70–72, 73, 74, 75, 77, 79–80, 81, 83, 86, 88, 96, 112, 119

Schulberg, Budd, 67, 75

Scripps-Howard chain, 81

Seamon, Mannie, 94, 105

Searcy State Hospital for the Colored Insane, 27

Sharkey, Jack, 20, 73, 74

Simms, Eddie, 74

Simon, Abe, 86, 96, 97

Soviet Union, 20

Spirit of Youth, The, 71

Spring Hill, 81, 91

Stinson, Henry L., 98, 100

Strauss, Sol, 108

Sun, 68

This Is the Army, 100–101

Toronto, Canada, 41

Tournament of Champions, 112

Trafton's gym, 45, 46, 47, 52

Trotter, Marva, 66–67, 70, 72, 84, 91, 94, 95, 98, 101, 103, 106, 108, 109, 112, 116, 118

Tunney, Gene, 20, 112

Twentieth Century Sporting Club, 57, 59, 81, 108

United States Army, 95–96, 99–102

Uzcudun, Paolino, 69, 71

Walcott, Jersey Joe, 109–12

Walsh McClean, Evalyn, 20, 22

War Department, 101

Washington, D.C., 100

Willard, Jess, 52

Williams, Holman, 40

Willkie, Wendell, 94

Woodward, Stanley, 25

World War II, 91, 93, 103

Yankee Stadium, 11, 12, 20, 59, 60, 65, 67, 69, 72, 73, 84, 85, 86, 105, 112–12, 113

PICTURE CREDITS

AP/Wide World Photos: pp. 15, 30, 35, 50, 70, 77, 90, 99, 104, 109, 120; Bettmann: pp. 47, 60, 89, 115; Culver Pictures, Inc.: pp. 9, 96, 102; *New York Daily News* Photo: pp. 29, 85; The Schomburg Center for Research in Black Culture/The New York Public Library, Astor, Lenox, and Tilden Foundation: p. 78; Smithsonian Institution, photo no. 87-15211-10: p. 18; UPI/Bettmann: pp. 8, 10, 12, 13, 17, 21, 25, 26, 38, 42, 45, 52, 55, 56, 62, 64, 67, 68, 71, 73, 74, 75, 76, 80, 83, 92, 95, 97, 101, 107, 111, 114, 117, 118, 119

ROBERT JAKOUBEK holds degrees in history from Indiana University and Columbia University. He is coauthor of *These United States*, an American history textbook published by Houghton Mifflin. He is also the author of *Martin Luther King, Jr.*, and *Adam Clayton Powell, Jr.*, in Chelsea House's BLACK AMERICANS OF ACHIEVEMENT series and *Harriet Beecher Stowe* in Chelsea's AMERICAN WOMEN OF ACHIEVEMENT series.

NATHAN IRVIN HUGGINS is W.E.B. Du Bois Professor of History and Director of the W.E.B. Du Bois Institute for Afro-American Research at Harvard University. He previously taught at Columbia University. Professor Huggins is the author of numerous books, including *Black Odyssey: The Afro-American Ordeal in Slavery*, *The Harlem Renaissance*, and *Slave and Citizen: The Life of Frederick Douglass*.